PREFACE

Welcome to “Mastering Algorithms and Data Structures”, a comprehensive guide designed to bridge the gap between theoretical concepts and practical application in the realm of computer science. This book is crafted for students, professionals, and enthusiasts who aspire to understand and master the intricacies of algorithms and Data Structures—essential pillars of efficient problem-solving in computing.

The content of this book is thoughtfully organized to ensure a holistic learning experience. Each chapter begins with a clear explanation of fundamental concepts, followed by detailed examples that highlight their real-world applications. To solidify understanding, we have included a variety of engaging exercises such as Multiple-Choice Questions (MCQs), "Match the Following" activities, and "Fill in the Blanks." These are complemented by in-depth case studies that illustrate how these concepts are applied to solve complex problems.

For those preparing for competitive exams or interviews, this book includes a curated collection of previous year questions and viva voce questions to help you test your readiness and confidence. Whether you are a beginner or someone with prior knowledge looking to refine your skills, this book is your companion for developing a structured approach to mastering algorithms and Data Structures.

As you journey through Mastering Algorithms and Data Structures, we encourage you to engage actively with the exercises and reflect on the case studies. By doing so, you will not only gain proficiency in the subject but also cultivate a problem-solving mindset that will serve you well in your academic, professional, and personal endeavors.

Table of Contents

Chapter 1 - Introduction to Data Structure And Algorithm

In this chapter you will learn about:

Definitions of DSA
Types of Data Structures
Primitive vs Non-Primitive Data Structures
Algorithmic Notations and Basic Concepts
Introduction to Algorithm Analysis
Time and Space Complexity
Big O, Ω, and Θ Notations

Data Structures and algorithms are the fundamental building blocks of computer science. They help us organize data in ways that make it easy to retrieve, manipulate, and use efficiently. Whether you're solving a complex problem or developing a system, the choice of Data Structures and algorithms can significantly impact performance, speed, and resource usage.

This chapter introduces core concepts of Data Structures and algorithms, providing an overview of how they function, their types, and how to analyze their efficiency. Through diagrams, code examples, and real-world applications, you'll gain a comprehensive understanding of how to use them effectively.

1.1 Definitions of Data Structures and Algorithms

Data Structures: These are specialized formats for organizing, storing, and managing data. Examples include arrays, linked lists, stacks, queues, trees, and graphs. The choice of Data Structure affects the efficiency of operations like searching, inserting, and deleting.

Algorithms: An algorithm is a step-by-step procedure or formula for solving a problem. They can be as simple as sorting a list or as complex as navigating a network of roads. The efficiency of an algorithm is measured by the time it takes to run (time complexity) and the amount of memory it uses (space complexity).

Example:

A common algorithm is binary search, which finds an element in a sorted list by repeatedly dividing the search interval in half.

1.2 Types of Data Structures

Data Structures are typically categorized as:

Primitive Data Structures: These are basic structures like integers, floats, and characters, which are the building blocks of more complex Data Structures.

Non-Primitive Data Structures: More complex structures, including:

- **Linear**: Data elements are arranged in a sequential manner (e.g., arrays, linked lists).
- **Non-linear**: Data elements are arranged hierarchically (e.g., trees, graphs).

1.3 Primitive vs. Non-Primitive Data Structures

- Primitive Data Structures: These include basic data types provided by programming languages like int, char, float.
- Non-Primitive Data Structures: These include advanced structures like arrays, linked lists, stacks, queues, trees, and graphs.
- Graphical Representation:A diagram showing an array (linear) vs. a tree (non-linear).

1.4 Algorithmic Notations and Basic Concepts

Algorithmic Notations: Notations like pseudocode or flowcharts are used to represent algorithms in a human-readable form. These notations simplify the understanding of an algorithm's steps.

Basic Concepts: Concepts like recursion, iteration, and greedy approaches are fundamental in designing algorithms.

Example:

A recursive algorithm for calculating the factorial of a number.

```
int factorial(int n) {
  if (n == 1) return 1;
```

```
    return n * factorial(n - 1);
}
```

1.5 Introduction to Algorithm Analysis

Algorithm analysis is critical to understanding the performance of algorithms. It involves:

- **Time Complexity**: Measures how the running time of an algorithm grows with the size of the input.
- **Space Complexity**: Measures the amount of memory an algorithm uses.

1.6 Time Complexity: Best, Worst, and Average Case

Time complexity tells us how fast an algorithm runs.

- **Best Case**: The minimum time an algorithm takes to complete (usually when the input is the most favorable).
- **Worst Case**: The maximum time an algorithm could take (often when input is least favorable).
- **Average Case**: The expected time for a random input.
- *Graphical Example*:
  - A **time complexity graph** showing the best, worst, and average cases for common algorithms like Bubble Sort, Quick Sort, and Merge Sort.

1.7 Space Complexity

Space complexity involves understanding how much memory an algorithm needs to execute. This includes:

- **Auxiliary space**: Extra space or temporary variables apart from the input size.
- **In-place algorithms**: Algorithms that use a constant amount of extra space.

1.8 Big O, Ω, and Θ Notations

These notations are used to express time and space complexity:

- **Big O (O)**: Describes the upper bound or worst-case scenario.
- **Omega (Ω)**: Describes the lower bound or best-case scenario.
- **Theta (Θ)**: Describes the average case or exact bound.
- *Example*:
- For a **binary search** algorithm, the time complexity is:
  - **O(log n)** in the worst case.
- A graph showcasing different growth rates (linear, logarithmic, quadratic) for various algorithms will help visualize these notations.

1.9 Glossary

- **Algorithm**: A set of well-defined instructions or procedures for solving a specific problem. Algorithms are used in programming to perform tasks like sorting, searching, and calculating. Example: Binary Search Algorithm for finding an element in a sorted array.
- **Data Structure**: A method for organizing and storing data so it can be accessed and modified efficiently. Examples include arrays, stacks, queues, linked lists, trees, and graphs.
- **Time Complexity**: A measure of the amount of time an algorithm takes to run relative to the size of the input data. It helps compare different algorithms based on their efficiency. Expressed using notations like Big O, it represents worst-case scenarios. For example, a linear search has O(n) time complexity.
- **Space Complexity**: The amount of memory space required by an algorithm to execute, often alongside time complexity. It includes both the input space and the additional space the algorithm uses during execution.
- **Big O Notation (O)**: Represents the upper bound of the time complexity, indicating the worst-case performance of an algorithm as the input size grows. For example, the time complexity of Bubble Sort is $O(n^2)$ in the worst case.
- **Omega Notation (Ω)**: Describes the best-case performance of an algorithm, providing the lower bound for the time it takes to run. For instance, the best-case time complexity of Quick Sort is Ω(n log n).

Theta Notation (Θ): Represents the exact bound or the average time complexity of an algorithm, covering both best and worst-case scenarios. If an algorithm takes approximately the same time in all cases, we use Θ.

Recursion: A method where a function calls itself to solve smaller instances of the same problem. It is often used in algorithms like the calculation of factorial or the Fibonacci sequence. Example: A recursive algorithm for computing factorial of a number n:

```
int factorial(int n) {
if (n == 1) return 1;
return n * factorial(n - 1);
}
```

Iteration: The repetition of a block of code a certain number of times, often using loops like for, while, or do-while. For example, iterating over an array to find the largest element.

In-place Algorithm: An algorithm that transforms the input without using additional memory proportional to the input size. Example: In-place sorting algorithms like Quick Sort or Bubble Sort.

Auxiliary Space: The extra space or temporary space used by an algorithm, apart from the input data. For instance, Merge Sort requires O(n) auxiliary space to store the temporary sub-arrays used during sorting.

1.10 Summary

- Data Structures are specialized formats for organizing and managing data efficiently.
- Algorithms are step-by-step procedures to solve specific problems.
- Data Structures can be categorized into primitive (basic types) and non-primitive (linear and non-linear) types.
- Algorithmic notations like pseudocode and flowcharts help in visualizing and writing algorithms.
- Algorithm analysis focuses on time complexity (best, worst, and average cases) and space complexity.
- Common notations for algorithm efficiency are Big O (worst case), Omega (best case), and Theta (average case).
- Understanding both time and space complexity is crucial for developing efficient algorithms.
- The upcoming chapters will explore specific Data Structures and algorithms in greater detail, supported by diagrams and code examples.

1.11 Previous Year Unsolved Questions

1. Explain the purpose of Big-O notation and compute the time complexity of the following loop: (RTU 2023-24)

```
for (int i=0; i<n; i==) cout << ”Current count = “<< I <<”\n”;
```

2. Define "Time Complexity" and "Space Complexity". What are the differences between them? (IGNOU 2021)
3. Compute time complexity of the following recurrence relation: (RTU 2023-24)

$$T(n) = T(n/3) + 1; \ T(1) = 1$$

4. What is dequeue? (Anna University 2013)
5. Using Separate Chaining Technique, Resolve Collision in the following Keys using function mod 9 and show the Data Structure:

   14, 11, 38, 50, 41, 7, 92, 182, 4.

   (RTU 2023-24)
6. What is meant by *Big-O* notation? Explain with an example. (IGNOU 2022)
7. What is the use of reference variable and static variable? Give example. (RTU 2023-24)
8. Write an algorithm that accepts two strings, S1 and S2, as input and then find whether S1 is a substring of S2. (IGNOU 2022)
9. What is an Abstract class? (IGNOU 2022)
10. What is Data Structure? Explain different Data Structures with example (Pune University 2019)

Exercises

Exercise 1 – Multiple Choice Questions

1. **What is a Data Structure?**
   A) A set of algorithms for solving a problem
   B) A way of organizing and storing data in a computer
   C) A programming language
   D) A type of software application
2. **Which of the following is an example of a linear Data Structure?**
   A) Tree
   B) Graph
   C) Linked List
   D) Hash Table

Exercise 2 – True/False

1. Data Structures are used solely for storing data, without any focus on data manipulation.
2. The time complexity of an algorithm is a measure of the amount of time it takes to execute, considering the worst-case scenario.

Exercise 3 – Fill in the blanks

1. A Data Structure that organizes data in a sequential order is known as a __________.
2. The __________ notation is used to describe the upper bound of an algorithm's running time.

Exercise 4- Fill in the blanks with two options

1. A _______ is a systematic way of organizing and managing data, while an _______ is a step-by-step procedure for solving a problem.
2. The time complexity of an algorithm is analyzed in terms of _______ and _______ cases to evaluate its efficiency.

Exercise 5- Rearrange the sentence

1. Importance / algorithms / in / of / structures / organizing / and / data / problem-solving
2. Different / structures / are / of / classifications / data / types / linear / non-linear / and.

Exercise 6- Choose the Odd One Out

1. Which one is the odd one out?
   A) Array
   B) Linked List
   C) Binary Tree
   D) Integer
2. Which one is the odd one out?
   A) Best Case
   B) Worst Case
   C) Average Case
   D) Space Complexity

Exercise 7- Jumble words

1. **Jumbled Word:** RGYOLHTMAI
2. **Jumbled Word:** RPEXOCMYL

Exercise 8- Match case

Column A

1. Data Structure
2. Algorithm
3. Time Complexity
4. Big O Notation

Column B
A. Notation to describe the upper bound of an algorithm's performance
B. Organizes and manages data for efficient access and modification
C. A step-by-step procedure to solve a specific problem
D. Measures the amount of time an algorithm takes to run

Exercise 9- Assertion – Reason

1. Assertion: Time complexity of an algorithm helps in determining the efficiency of an algorithm.
Reason: Time complexity measures the amount of memory space required by an algorithm during its execution.
a) Both Assertion and Reason are correct explanation for Assertion.
b) Both Assertion and Reason but Reason is the correct explanation for Assertion.
c) Assertion is correct, but Reason is incorrect.
d) Assertion is incorrect, but Reason is correct.

Exercise 10- Read the questions given below and find the appropriate word in the grid provided.

A	R	R	A	Y	N	O	P	Q
H	W	E	T	R	I	Y	J	L
D	K	S	T	A	C	K	U	V
P	M	O	L	P	H	E	S	G
F	A	E	C	R	T	N	F	W
Q	I	B	T	D	G	L	S	Z
L	X	M	S	K	I	Y	T	M

Find the following words in the grid:
1. Array
2. Stack

Exercise 11- One- word
1. What notation is used to describe the upper bound of an algorithm's time complexity?
2. What is the simplest type of Data Structure that consists of elements stored in a linear order?

Exercise 12- Small Answers
1. What is Data Structure, and why is it important in computer science?
2. Differentiate between primitive and non-primitive Data Structures.

Exercise 13- Long Answers
1. Explain the different types of Data Structures and their significance in computer science.
2. Discuss the concepts of time complexity and space complexity in algorithm analysis. Provide examples of each.

Answers

Exercise 1-

1. B) A way of organizing and storing data in a computer, 2. C) Linked List

Exercise 2-

1. False, 2. True

Exercise 3-

1. linear Data Structure, 2. Big O

Exercise 4-

1. Data Structure, algorithm, 2. best, worst

Exercise 5-

1. Importance of Data Structures and algorithms in organizing and problem-solving.
2. Different classifications of Data Structures are linear and non-linear types.

Exercise 6-

1. D) Integer, 2. D) Space Complexity

Exercise 7-

1. ALGORITHM, 2. COMPLEXITY

Exercise 8-

1-B, 2-C, 3-D, 4-A

Exercise 9-

1. c) Assertion is correct, but Reason is incorrect.

Exercise 11-

1. Big O, 2. Array

Test Paper

Chapter-1
Introduction to Data Structure And Algorithm

Time Duration: 30 Minutes **Maximum Marks: 25**

General Instructions:

1. The question paper consists of 12 questions and is divided into four sections, A, B, C and D.
2. All questions are compulsory.
3. Section A comprises MCQs, Fill in the blanks and True or False carrying one marks each.
4. Section B comprises VSAQs(very short answers questions) carrying two marks each.
5. Section C comprises SAQs(short questions) carrying four marks each.
6. Section D comprises long questions carrying five marks each.

SECTION-A

I. Multiple choice questions: **(1*2=2)**

1. What does Big O notation describe in algorithm analysis?
A) The actual running time of an algorithm
B) The average case complexity of an algorithm
C) The upper bound of an algorithm's running time
D) The amount of memory an algorithm uses

2. Which of the following best describes time complexity?
A) The amount of memory required by an algorithm
B) The speed at which an algorithm runs
C) The number of operations an algorithm performs
D) The amount of time taken to write the algorithm relative to the input size

II. True or False: **(1*2=2)**

1. Arrays and linked lists are examples of non-linear Data Structures.
2. Primitive Data Structures are built using non-primitive Data Structures.

III. Fill in the blanks: **(1*2=2)**

1. In a _______________ Data Structure, each element points to the next, forming a sequence, as seen in linked lists.
2. The process of evaluating the efficiency of an algorithm based on its time and space requirements is known as ___________.

SECTION-B

IV. Very Short answers type questions I **(2*3=6)**

1. Which type of Data Structure allows elements to be added or removed only from one end?
2. What is the term for the memory usage of an algorithm?
3. What is a common graphical tool used to represent the steps in an algorithm?

SECTION-C

V. Short answers type questions-II **(4*2=8)**

1. What is time complexity, and why is it important to analyze it?
2. Explain the difference between Big O, Omega (Ω), and Theta (Θ) notations.

SECTION-D

VI. Long answers type questions **(5*1=5)**

1. What are Big O, Ω (Omega), and Θ (Theta) notations? Explain their significance with examples.

Chapter 2 - Arrays and Linked Lists

In this chapter you will learn about:
Arrays
Single and Multi-Dimensional Arrays
Sparse Matrices
Introduction to Linked Lists
Singly Linked List
Doubly Linked List
Circular Linked List
Memory Representation of Linked Lists
Applications of Linked Lists

In computer science, Data Structures are the backbone of efficient algorithms and system design. Arrays and linked lists are among the most fundamental and widely used Data Structures. Arrays offer constant-time access to elements through indexing, making them ideal for scenarios where the size of data is known and fixed. On the other hand, linked lists provide flexibility by dynamically allocating memory, which allows for efficient insertions and deletions without memory constraints. This chapter dives deep into arrays and linked lists, discussing their concepts, operations, and applications, complete with diagrams, example programs, and visual representations.

2.1 Arrays: Concepts and Operations

Arrays are linear Data Structures that store elements in contiguous memory locations. They provide efficient access to data through indexing, but their size is fixed upon initialization. Common operations associated with arrays include:

- **Traversal**: Accessing each element one by one.
- **Insertion**: Adding an element at a specific position (involves shifting existing elements).
- **Deletion**: Removing an element and shifting the remaining elements.
- **Searching**: Finding an element through linear or binary search techniques.

Example Program (Array Traversal):

```
#include <stdio.h>
int main() {
   int arr[5] = {10, 20, 30, 40, 50};
   for(int i = 0; i < 5; i++) {
      printf("%d ", arr[i]);
   }
   return 0;
}
```

In the above code, the array arr stores five elements, and we traverse the array to print its contents.

2.2 Single and Multi-Dimensional Arrays

Single-dimensional arrays represent data in a single line, while multi-dimensional arrays (e.g., 2D arrays) represent data in a grid or matrix form, allowing for more complex Data Structures.
For example, a 2D array representing a matrix:

```
int matrix[3][3] = {
   {1, 2, 3},
   {4, 5, 6},
   {7, 8, 9}
};
```

Here, matrix is a 3x3 array, representing rows and columns.

Operations on Arrays:

- Accessing elements via row and column indices.
- Performing matrix operations like addition, subtraction, or multiplication.

2.3 Sparse Matrices: Representation and Applications

A sparse matrix is one in which most elements are zero. Storing sparse matrices using traditional arrays would waste memory. Specialized storage techniques like Compressed Sparse Row (CSR) or Coordinate List (COO) efficiently store only non-zero elements.

Applications of Sparse Matrices:

Graph Algorithms: Where adjacency matrices are sparse.

Scientific Computing: Used in simulations and optimizations where zeroes dominate the data set.

2.4 Introduction to Linked Lists

A linked list is a linear Data Structure where elements are connected by pointers. Each node consists of two parts:

Data: The value stored in the node.

Pointer: A reference to the next node in the list.

Linked lists allow dynamic memory allocation and are efficient for applications that involve frequent insertions and deletions, as they do not require shifting elements.

2.5 Singly Linked List: Structure and Operations

A singly linked list is a list where each node points to the next node, and the last node points to NULL, indicating the end of the list.

Operations on Singly Linked Lists:

Insertion: Nodes can be inserted at the head, tail, or any position.

Deletion: Removing nodes from any position.

Traversal: Accessing and displaying all nodes.

Example Program (Singly Linked List Creation):

```
#include <stdio.h>
#include <stdlib.h>

struct Node {
   int data;
   struct Node* next;
};

void printList(struct Node* n) {
   while (n != NULL) {
      printf("%d ", n->data);
      n = n->next;
   }
}

int main() {
   struct Node* head = NULL;
   struct Node* second = NULL;
   struct Node* third = NULL;
```

```c
    // Allocate memory for nodes in the linked list
    head = (struct Node*)malloc(sizeof(struct Node));
    second = (struct Node*)malloc(sizeof(struct Node));
    third = (struct Node*)malloc(sizeof(struct Node));

    // Assign data to nodes
    head->data = 1;
    head->next = second;
    second->data = 2;
    second->next = third;
    third->data = 3;
    third->next = NULL;

    // Print the linked list
    printList(head);

    return 0;
}
```

This program creates a simple singly linked list and prints its elements.

2.6 Doubly Linked List: Structure and Operations

In a doubly linked list, each node contains two pointers: one pointing to the next node and another pointing to the previous node. This allows for traversal in both directions—forward and backward.

Advantages of Doubly Linked Lists:

- Easier to implement operations that require traversal in both directions.
- Efficient for operations such as inserting or deleting nodes from both ends.

2.7 Circular Linked List: Structure and Operations

A circular linked list is a linked list where the last node points back to the first node, forming a circle. Circular linked lists can be singly or doubly linked.

Applications:

Round-robin scheduling: Where processes are executed in a cyclic order.
Buffer management: Where continuous cycling through a set of data is required.

2.8 Memory Representation of Linked Lists

Unlike arrays, linked lists do not require contiguous memory allocation. Each node is dynamically allocated as needed, leading to more efficient use of memory when the data size changes frequently. However, they consume additional memory due to pointers.

Comparison of Memory Use:

Arrays: Fixed size; more efficient for large blocks of data.
Linked Lists: Flexible size; better for applications requiring dynamic memory allocation.

2.9 Applications of Linked Lists

Linked lists are widely used in scenarios where dynamic memory allocation and flexibility are needed. Common applications include:

Stacks and Queues: Linked lists allow efficient implementation without the need for resizing.
Graph Representations: Adjacency lists, where each vertex points to a list of adjacent vertices.

Memory Management: Free lists in dynamic memory allocation systems use linked lists to track free memory blocks.
Undo Operations: Many software systems use linked lists to implement undo functionality.

2.10 Glossary

Array: A collection of elements stored in contiguous memory locations.
Linked List: A sequence of nodes, each containing data and a pointer to the next node.
Node: The basic unit of a linked list, consisting of data and a reference to the next node.
Sparse Matrix: A matrix in which most elements are zero, typically stored using specialized techniques.
Singly Linked List: A linked list where each node points to the next node only.
Doubly Linked List: A linked list where each node points to both the next and previous nodes.
Circular Linked List: A linked list where the last node points back to the first, forming a loop.

2.11 Summary

Arrays: Linear Data Structures with contiguous memory allocation, allowing fast access via indexing.
Single and Multi-Dimensional Arrays: Single-dimensional arrays store data in a linear form, while multi-dimensional arrays (like matrices) store data in grids or tables.
Sparse Matrices: Specialized representation for matrices with mostly zero elements to save memory.
Linked Lists: Dynamic Data Structures where each element (node) points to the next, offering flexibility in memory allocation.
Singly Linked Lists: Nodes point only to the next node, allowing one-way traversal.
Doubly Linked Lists: Nodes contain two pointers, one to the next and one to the previous node, allowing two-way traversal.
Circular Linked Lists: The last node points back to the first node, forming a circular structure, useful in cyclic processes.
Memory Representation: Linked lists use dynamic, non-contiguous memory allocation, which is more flexible than arrays but requires additional space for pointers.
Applications: Linked lists are commonly used in stacks, queues, graph adjacency lists, dynamic memory management, and undo operations in software systems.

2.12 Previous Year Unsolved Questions

1. Write an algorithm to insert an element into a singly linked list. Make necessary assumptions.
   (IGNOU 2022)
2. Write algorithm to convert an adjacency matrix representation of a sparse matrix to array storage representation of sparse matrix. write output after each pass of the Bubble Sort on the following data:
   (RTU 2023-24)
   72, 98, 61, 12, 6, 103, 71, 97
3. Write an algorithm for addition of two matrices.
   (IGNOU 2021)
4. What are multi-dimensional arrays? Explain roe major and column major representation of array storage.
   (Pune University 2019)
5. Elaborate the disadvantages of Linked List over Arrays.
   (RTU 2023-24)
6. Explain the concept of linear and nonlinear Data Structures with example.
   (Pune University 2019)
7. Examine each step involved with Radix sort to sort the given array:
   (RTU 2023-24)
   329,457,657,839, 436, 720, 355
8. What are Singly Linked Lists? Write an algorithm for implementation of a Singly Linked List.
   (IGNOU 2022)
9. (a)Write à program to perform the following operations on the Singly linked list:
   (MU 2022-23)
   I. Insert a node at the end

II. Delete a node from the beginning
III. Search for a given element in the list
IV. Display the list

(b) Write a C program to implement Stack using Linked List.

10. Write a function to delete the last node of the circular linked list.
(MU 2022-23)

Exercise

Exercise 1 – Multiple Choice Questions

1. Which of the following is true about arrays?
   A) Arrays store elements in contiguous memory locations
   B) Arrays are dynamic in size
   C) Arrays allow insertion at any position in O(1) time
   D) Arrays don't support random access
2. What is the time complexity to insert an element at the beginning of an array?
   A) O(1)
   B) O(log n)
   C) O(n)
   D) O(n^2)

Exercise 2 – True/False

1. An array is a collection of elements stored at non-contiguous memory locations.
2. In a linked list, each node points to the next node in the sequence.

Exercise 3 – Fill in the blanks

1. In an array, elements are stored in __________ memory locations.
2. The time complexity for accessing an element in an array by index is __________.

Exercise 4- Fill in the blanks with two options

1. In a doubly linked list, each node contains two pointers, one pointing to the __________ node and another pointing to the __________ node.
2. Arrays have a __________ size, whereas linked lists can __________ in size dynamically.

Exercise 5- Rearrange the sentence

1. Linked / in / memory / contiguous / elements / arrays / store
2. Singly / forward / traversed / linked / can / list / only / be

Exercise 6- Choose the Odd One Out

1. Which one is the odd one out?
   A) Array
   B) Stack
   C) Linked List
   D) Queue
2. Which one is the odd one out?
   A) Circular Linked List
   B) Singly Linked List
   C) Doubly Linked List
   D) Hash Table

Exercise 7- Jumble words

1. ERMITORFAP
2. EPNAIROLATIR

Exercise 8- Match case

Column A

1. Circular Linked List
2. Array
3. Singly Linked List
4. Doubly Linked List

Column B
A. Random access to elements
B. Pointers to both next and previous node
C. Fixed size, contiguous memory
D. Last node points to the first node

Exercise 9- Assertion – Reason

1. Assertion: Arrays have a fixed size.
Reason: Arrays allocate contiguous memory space for elements, which restricts their size after allocation.
a) Both Assertion and Reason are correct explanation for Assertion.
b) Both Assertion and Reason but Reason is the correct explanation for Assertion.
c) Assertion is correct, but Reason is incorrect.
d) Assertion is incorrect, but Reason is correct.

Exercise 10- Read the questions given below and find the appropriate word in the grid provided.

M	E	M	O	R	Y	Q	L	M
H	W	T	N	O	D	E	J	K
D	K	S	L	T	A	C	I	V
P	M	O	L	N	D	O	S	G
F	A	E	C	A	T	N	F	W
Q	I	B	T	D	G	L	S	Z
L	X	M	S	K	I	Y	T	M

Find the following words in the grid:
1. Memory
2. Node

Exercise 11- One- word

1. What Data Structure is used to store elements in contiguous memory locations?
2. What is the pointer in a singly linked list that points to the next node called?

Exercise 12- Small Answers

1. What is the primary difference between an array and a linked list?
2. Explain the main advantage of a circular linked list.

Exercise 13- Long Answers

1. Explain the key differences between arrays and linked lists. Discuss their advantages, disadvantages, and use cases.
2. Discuss the different types of linked lists and their respective advantages and disadvantages.

Answers

Exercise 1-

1. A) Arrays store elements in contiguous memory locations, 2. C) O(n)

Exercise 2-

1. False, 2. True

Exercise 3-

1. contiguous, 2. O (1)

Exercise 4-

1. previous, next, 2. fixed, grow

Exercise 5-

1. Arrays store elements in contiguous memory., 2. Singly linked list can only be traversed forward.

Exercise 6-

1. A) Array, 2. D) Hash Table

Exercise 7-

1. PERFORMANCE, 2. RELATIONAL

Exercise 8-

1-D, 2-C, 3-A, 4-B

Exercise 9-

1. b) Both Assertion and Reason but Reason is the correct explanation for Assertion.

Exercise 11-

1. Array, 2. Next

Test Paper
Chapter-2
Arrays and Linked Lists

Time Duration: 30 Minutes **Maximum Marks: 25**

General Instructions:

1. The question paper consists of 12 questions and is divided into four sections, A, B, C and D.
2. All questions are compulsory.
3. Section A comprises MCQs, Fill in the blanks and True or False carrying one marks each.
4. Section B comprises VSAQs(very short answers questions) carrying two marks each.
5. Section C comprises SAQs(short questions) carrying four marks each.
6. Section D comprises long questions carrying five marks each.

SECTION-A

I. Multiple choice questions: **(1*2=2)**

1. In a linked list, what is the time complexity to access the nth element?
   A) O(1)
   B) O(n)
   C) O(log n)
   D) O(n^2)
2. What is a key advantage of a doubly linked list over a singly linked list?
   A) Requires less memory
   B) Allows traversal in both directions
   C) Easier to implement
   D) No null pointer at the end

II. Fill in the blanks:
(1*2=2)

1. In a singly linked list, each node contains data and a __________ to the next node.
2. A circular linked list is a type of linked list where the last node points to the __________ node.

III. True or False:
(1*2=2)

1. A circular linked list allows for continuous traversal from the head to the tail without null reference.
2. Inserting an element at the end of a singly linked list is faster than doing the same in an array.

SECTION-B

IV. Very Short answers type questions-I **(2*3=6)**

1. Which type of linked list allows traversal in both directions?
2. What is the time complexity for inserting an element at the beginning of an array?
3. What kind of Data Structure is a list where the last element points back to the first element?

SECTION-C

V. Short answers type questions-II **(4*2=8)**

1. What are the two pointers in a doubly linked list?
2. Why is accessing an element in a linked list slower than in an array?

SECTION-D

VI. Long answers type questions **(5*1=5)**

1. What is the process of inserting and deleting an element in a linked list? Explain with examples for both singly and doubly linked
   lists.

Chapter 3 - Stack

In this chapter you will learn about:
Introduction to Stacks
Stack ADT
Stack Implementation using Arrays
Stack Implementation using Linked Lists
Application of Stack
Infix to Postfix Conversion
Evaluating Arithmetic Expressions
Simulating Recursion with Stacks
Tower of Hanoi using Stacks

In Data Structures, a stack is a linear structure that follows the Last In, First Out (LIFO) principle. This means that the last element added to the stack is the first one to be removed. Stacks are widely used in various algorithms and applications such as expression evaluation, parsing, and memory management. This chapter delves into the concepts, operations, and practical implementations of stacks using both arrays and linked lists, alongside various applications like infix to postfix conversion, expression evaluation, and the Tower of Hanoi problem.

3.1 Introduction to Stacks

A stack is an abstract data type (ADT) where elements are added (pushed) and removed (popped) from the top of the stack. Key operations in a stack include:

- **Push**: Add an element to the top.
- **Pop**: Remove the element from the top.
- **Peek (Top)**: Retrieve the top element without removing it.
- **IsEmpty**: Check whether the stack is empty.

Stacks have numerous real-world applications, such as in undo functionality, syntax parsing, and recursive function calls.

3.2 Stack ADT: Concepts and Operations

The Stack ADT supports the following core operations:

- **Push(element)**: Inserts an element onto the stack.
- **Pop()**: Removes the top element from the stack.
- **Peek()**: Returns the top element without modifying the stack.
- **IsEmpty()**: Checks if the stack contains no elements.
- **IsFull()**: Checks if the stack has reached its capacity (in a fixed-size stack implementation).

3.3 Stack Implementation using Arrays

An array-based stack uses a fixed-size array to store elements. It is simple to implement but has a limitation of static memory allocation.

Example Program (Stack Implementation using Array):

```
#include <stdio.h>
#define MAX 5

int stack[MAX];
int to p = -1;

void push(int value) {
  if (top == MAX - 1) {
    printf("Stack Overflow\n");
  } else {
    top++;
    stack[top] = value;
```

```
    }
}

int pop() {
    if (top == -1) {
        printf("Stack Underflow\n");
        return -1;
    } else {
        int value = stack[top];
        top--;
        return value;
    }
}

int peek() {
    if (top != -1) {
        return stack[top];
    } else {
        printf("Stack is empty\n");
        return -1;
    }
}

int main() {
    push(10);
    push(20);
    printf("Top element is %d\n", peek());
    pop();
    printf("Top element after pop is %d\n", peek());
    return 0;
}
```

3.4 Stack Implementation using Linked Lists

A dynamic stack can be implemented using a linked list, where each node points to the next element. This approach allows dynamic memory allocation and avoids the fixed size limitation of array-based stacks.

Example Program (Stack Implementation using Linked List):

```
#include <stdio.h>
#include <stdlib.h>

struct Node {
    int data;
    struct Node* next;
};

struct Node* top = NULL;

void push(int value) {
    struct Node* newNode = (struct Node*)malloc(sizeof(struct Node));
    if (!newNode) {
        printf("Heap Overflow\n");
        return;
    }
    newNode->data = value;
    newNode->next = top;
    top = newNode;
```

```
}

int pop() {
    if (top == NULL) {
        printf("Stack Underflow\n");
        return -1;
    } else {
        struct Node* temp = top;
        int value = top->data;
        top = top->next;
        free(temp);
        return value;
    }
}

int peek() {
    if (top != NULL) {
        return top->data;
    } else {
        printf("Stack is empty\n");
        return -1;
    }
}

int main() {
    push(10);
    push(20);
    printf("Top element is %d\n", peek());
    pop();
    printf("Top element after pop is %d\n", peek());
    return 0;
}
```

3.5 Applications of Stacks

Stacks are used in various computational problems and algorithms, including:

- **Expression evaluation**: Converting and evaluating infix, postfix, and prefix expressions.
- **Syntax parsing**: Used in compilers to check balanced parentheses or to parse expressions.
- **Function calls**: Stacks are used for storing local variables and function calls in recursion.
- **Undo operations**: In software applications like text editors, undo functionality is implemented using stacks.

3.6 Infix to Postfix Conversion

Infix expressions (where operators appear between operands) are easier for humans to understand, but postfix expressions (where operators appear after operands) are easier for machines to evaluate using stacks. The conversion can be done using the Shunting Yard Algorithm developed by Edsger Dijkstra.

Example:
Infix: A + B * C Postfix: A B C * +
A stack is used to temporarily store operators during the conversion.

3.7 Evaluating Arithmetic Expressions

Postfix expressions can be easily evaluated using a stack. Operands are pushed onto the stack, and when an operator is encountered, the necessary number of operands is popped, the operation is performed, and the result is pushed back onto the stack.

Example Program (Evaluating Postfix Expression):

```c
#include <stdio.h>
#include <ctype.h>

int stack[20];
int top = -1;

void push(int value) {
   stack[++top] = value;
}
int pop() {
   return stack[top--];
}
int evaluatePostfix(char* exp) {
   int i;
   for (i = 0; exp[i]; ++i) {
      if (isdigit(exp[i]))
         push(exp[i] - '0');
      else {
         int val1 = pop();
         int val2 = pop();
         switch (exp[i]) {
            case '+': push(val2 + val1); break;
            case '-': push(val2 - val1); break;
            case '*': push(val2 * val1); break;
            case '/': push(val2 / val1); break;
         }
      }
   }
   return pop();
}

int main() {
   char exp[] = "231*+9-";
   printf("Postfix Evaluation: %d\n", evaluatePostfix(exp));
   return 0;
}
```

3.8 Simulating Recursion with Stacks

Recursion uses the system's call stack to keep track of function calls. However, recursion can be simulated manually using an explicit stack Data Structure, which can help avoid deep recursion and stack overflow errors.

3.9 Tower of Hanoi using Stacks

The Tower of Hanoi is a classic problem where three pegs and a set of disks of different sizes are used. The objective is to move the disks from one peg to another, with certain rules. Stacks can be used to simulate the movement of disks in an iterative solution, avoiding recursive function calls.

3.10 Glossary

Stack: A linear Data Structure that follows LIFO (Last In, First Out) ordering.
Push: Operation to add an element to the top of the stack.
Pop: Operation to remove the top element from the stack.
Peek (Top): Operation to access the top element without removing it.
Postfix Expression: A mathematical notation where operators follow the operands.

3.11 Summary

Stack: A linear Data Structure that follows the Last In, First Out (LIFO) principle.

Key Operations:

- Push: Adds an element to the top of the stack.
- Pop: Removes the top element.
- Peek: Retrieves the top element without removing it.
- IsEmpty: Checks if the stack is empty.

Stack Implementation:

- Using Arrays: Simple, fixed-size stack with array storage.
- Using Linked Lists: Dynamically sized stack with linked list nodes.

Applications of Stacks:

- Expression evaluation (infix to postfix).
- Function call management (recursion).
- Undo operations in software (e.g., text editors).

Infix to Postfix Conversion: Converts human-readable infix expressions to machine-friendly postfix expressions using a stack.

Evaluating Postfix Expressions: Operands are pushed onto a stack, and operators are applied to operands popped from the stack.

Simulating Recursion: Stacks can simulate recursion in an iterative way, avoiding system stack overflow.

Tower of Hanoi: Stacks can be used to solve the Tower of Hanoi problem iteratively.

3.12 Previous Year Unsolved Questions

1. Define "Stack". Explain the operations that can be performed on a stack. (IGNOU 2021)
2. Where the stack Data Structures are used in sequential organization? Explain with example. (Pune University 2013)
3. Identify the applications of stack. (RTU 2023-24)
4. Convert the following infix expression into postfix expression (RTU 2023-24)

   A+B-(C+D)/EF-(GH)/1
5. What is a Stack? Write an algorithm for implementation of a Stack. (IGNOU 2022)
6. Evaluate the following postfix expression using stack. 76 2451-/- (RTU 2023-24)
7. Convert the following expression to postfix. (MU 2022-23)

   (f-g) * ((a+b) * (c-d))/e
8. The equivalent postfix expression corresponding to the infix expression (A+B) *(D/C) is (MU 2022-23)

   A.) ABDC/*+
   B.) AB+D*C/
   C.) AB+DC/*
   D.) ABD*+C/
9. Explain the operations that are performed on Stacks. Write an algorithm to push an element to the stack. (IGNOU 2022)

Exercises

Exercise 1 – Multiple Choice Questions

1. What is the most common operation performed on a stack?
    A) Enqueue
    B) Push
    C) Insert
    D) Append
2. Stacks follow which order of operation?
    A) First In First Out (FIFO)
    B) Last In First Out (LIFO)
    C) Random Order
    D) Priority Based

Exercise 2 – True/False

1. Stacks use First In First Out (FIFO) order for their operations.
2. The push operation adds an element to the top of the stack.

Exercise 3 – Fill in the blanks

1. Stacks follow the __________ order of operation.
2. The operation used to add an element to a stack is called __________.

Exercise 4- Fill in the blanks with two options

1. A stack Data Structure operates on a _______ principle, where elements are added using the __________ operation.
2. In a stack, removing an element is called a __________ operation, and trying to remove an element from an empty stack causes __________.

Exercise 5- Rearrange the sentence

1. Operation / stack / first / a / in / is / the / added / element / last / removed / the / one.
2. Occurs / stack / the / of / when / full / overflow / is / condition / a.

Exercise 6- Choose the Odd One Out

1. Which one is the odd one out?
    A) Push
    B) Pop
    C) Enqueue
    D) Peek

2. Which one is the odd one out?
    A) Overflow
    B) Underflow
    C) LIFO
    D) FIFO

Exercise 7- Jumble words

1. FIOL
2. PHUS

Exercise 8- Match case

Column A

1. Push
2. Pop
3. Peek

4. Underflow
5. Overflow

Column B
A. Removes the top element of the stack
B. Adds an element to the top of the stack
C. The top element is accessed without removal
D. Occurs when attempting to pop from an empty stack
E. Happens when a stack is full

Exercise 9- Assertion – Reason

1. **Assertion**: A stack follows the LIFO principle.
   Reason: In a stack, the last element added is the first one to be removed.
   a) Both Assertion and Reason are correct explanation for Assertion.
   b) Both Assertion and Reason but Reason is the correct explanation for Assertion.
   c) Assertion is correct, but Reason is incorrect.
   d) Assertion is incorrect, but Reason is correct.

Exercise 10- Read the questions given below and find the appropriate word in the grid provided.

P	O	P	B	H	U	S	H	Q
K	L	Q	T	R	E	D	M	N
D	A	B	W	I	S	H	O	P
O	T	A	C	K	U	R	F	S
H	A	R	E	Q	L	J	A	W
G	I	S	P	U	S	H	Z	M
M	T	R	Y	P	H	T	K	N

Find the following words in the grid:

1. Push
2. Pop

Exercise 11- One- word

1. What principle does a stack follow?
2. Which operation adds an element to the top of a stack?

Exercise 12- Small Answers

1. What is a stack, and how does it work?
2. What is the difference between "push" and "pop" operations in a stack?

Exercise 13- Long Answers

1. Explain the working of a stack with its operations (Push, Pop, Peek) using an example.
2. What are the common applications of stacks in real-world scenarios? Explain any three with examples.

Answers

Exercise 1-

1. B) Push, 2. B) Last in First Out (LIFO)

Exercise 2-

1. False, 2. True

Exercise 3-

1. LIFO, 2. Push

Exercise 4-

1. LIFO, Push, 2. Pop, Underflow

Exercise 5-

1. In a stack, the first element added is the last one removed, 2. Overflow occurs when a stack is full.

Exercise 6-

1. Enqueue, 2. FIFO

Exercise 7-

1. LIFO, 2. PUSH

Exercise 9-

1-B,2-A,3-C,4-D,5-E

Exercise 9-

1. b) Both Assertion and Reason but Reason is the correct explanation for Assertion.

Exercise 11-

1. LIFO, 2. Push

Test Paper

Chapter-3
Stack

Time Duration: 30 Minutes **Maximum Marks: 25**

General Instructions:
1. The question paper consists of 12 questions and is divided into four sections, A, B, C and D.
2. All questions are compulsory.
3. Section A comprises MCQs, Fill in the blanks and True or False carrying one marks each.
4. Section B comprises VSAQs(very short answers questions) carrying two marks each.
5. Section C comprises SAQs(short questions) carrying four marks each.
6. Section D comprises long questions carrying five marks each.

SECTION-A

I. Multiple choice questions: **(1*2=2)**

1. Which of the following is not an application of stack?
   A) Function call management in recursion
   B) Parsing in compilers
   C) Scheduling tasks in an operating system
   D) Evaluating mathematical expressions
2. Which operation is used to remove the top element of a stack?
   A) Push
   B) Pop
   C) Peek
   D) Insert

II. Fill in the blanks: **(1*2=2)**

1. The __________ operation returns the top element of a stack without removing it.
2. A stack Data Structure can be efficiently used for managing __________ calls in recursion.

III. True or False: **(1*2=2)**

1. In stacks, you can access elements in the middle without removing the top elements.
2. A stack can be implemented using arrays or linked lists.

SECTION-B

IV. Very Short answers type questions-I **(2*3=6)**

1. What is the term for removing the top element of a stack?
2. What is it called when you try to pop from an empty stack?
3. Which operation returns the top element without removing it?

SECTION-C

V. Short answers type questions-II **(4*2=8)**

1. What is overflow in a stack?
2. What are some real-life applications of stacks?

SECTION-D

VI. Long answers type questions **(5*1=5)**

1. Discuss the conditions of Overflow and Underflow in a stack. How can these conditions be managed in practical applications?

Chapter 4 - Queues

In this chapter you will learn about:
Introduction to Queues
Queue ADT
Queue Implementation using Arrays
Queue Implementation using Linked Lists
Circular Queue
Application of Queues
Dequeue and Priority Queue
Round Robin Scheduling
Job Scheduling using Queues

A queue is a linear Data Structure that follows the First In, First Out (FIFO) principle, meaning the first element added to the queue is the first one to be removed. Queues are essential in various computational problems and systems, including operating system process scheduling, network traffic handling, and simulation of real-world queues such as waiting lines. This chapter covers the concepts, operations, and implementations of queues, including circular queues, priority queues, and dequeues. Several applications and scheduling algorithms, such as Round Robin and Job Scheduling, are explored in detail.

4.1 Introduction to Queues

A queue allows insertion of elements at the rear and removal of elements from the front. This makes it ideal for scenarios like processing tasks in the order they arrive. The primary operations associated with queues include:

- **Enqueue**: Adding an element to the rear.
- **Dequeue**: Removing an element from the front.
- **Peek (Front)**: Retrieving the front element without removing it.
- **IsEmpty**: Checking whether the queue is empty.

4.2 Queue ADT: Concepts and Operations

The Queue Abstract Data Type (ADT) supports the following fundamental operations:

- **Enqueue(element)**: Inserts an element at the rear of the queue.
- **Dequeue()**: Removes the element at the front of the queue.
- **Peek()**: Returns the front element without modifying the queue.
- **IsEmpty()**: Returns true if the queue is empty.
- **IsFull()**: In a fixed-size queue, returns true if the queue is full.

4.3 Queue Implementation using Arrays

An array-based implementation of a queue uses a fixed-size array where two pointers (front and rear) are maintained to keep track of the positions for insertion and deletion. However, after a certain number of operations, the front may move forward, leaving unused space at the start of the array, which can be inefficient.

Example Program (Queue Implementation using Array):

```
#include <stdio.h>
#define MAX 5

int queue[MAX];
int front = -1, rear = -1;

void enqueue(int value) {
   if (rear == MAX - 1) {
      printf("Queue Overflow\n");
   } else {
      if (front == -1) front = 0;
      rear++;
```

```
        queue[rear] = value;
    }
}

int dequeue() {
    if (front == -1 || front > rear) {
        printf("Queue Underflow\n");
        return -1;
    } else {
        int value = queue[front];
        front++;
        return value;
    }
}

int peek() {
    if (front != -1 && front <= rear) {
        return queue[front];
    } else {
        printf("Queue is empty\n");
        return -1;
    }
}

int main() {
    enqueue(10);
    enqueue(20);
    printf("Front element is %d\n", peek());
    dequeue();
    printf("Front element after dequeue is %d\n", peek());
    return 0;
}
```

4.4 Queue Implementation using Linked Lists

A linked list-based implementation provides a dynamic queue where nodes are created as needed, avoiding the fixed size limitation of arrays. This makes it more flexible for scenarios where the number of elements is not known in advance.

Example Program (Queue Implementation using Linked List):

```
#include <stdio.h>
#include <stdlib.h>

struct Node {
    int data;
    struct Node* next;
};

struct Node* front = NULL;
struct Node* rear = NULL;

void enqueue(int value) {
    struct Node* newNode = (struct Node*)malloc(sizeof(struct Node));
    newNode->data = value;
    newNode->next = NULL;
    if (rear == NULL) {
        front = rear = newNode;
```

```
    } else {
        rear->next = newNode;
        rear = newNode;
    }
}

int dequeue() {
    if (front == NULL) {
        printf("Queue Underflow\n");
        return -1;
    } else {
        struct Node* temp = front;
        int value = front->data;
        front = front->next;
        if (front == NULL) rear = NULL;
        free(temp);
        return value;
    }
}

int peek() {
    if (front != NULL) {
        return front->data;
    } else {
        printf("Queue is empty\n");
        return -1;
    }
}

int main() {
    enqueue(10);
    enqueue(20);
    printf("Front element is %d\n", peek());
    dequeue();
    printf("Front element after dequeue is %d\n", peek());
    return 0;
}
```

4.5 Circular Queue: Concepts and Operations

A circular queue is a queue where the last position connects back to the first, forming a circle. This solves the problem of unused space in a linear array implementation by allowing the rear pointer to wrap around to the beginning once the array is full. Circular queues are ideal for applications like buffering in streaming systems.

Example (Circular Queue Illustration):

Initial: Front = 0, Rear = 0
Enqueue: Front = 0, Rear = 1
Wrap-around: Rear = 0 (after reaching the end of the array)

4.6 Dequeue and Priority Queue: Concepts and Operations

Dequeue (Double-Ended Queue): In a dequeue, elements can be inserted or removed from both the front and rear, providing greater flexibility.

Priority Queue: In a priority queue, each element is associated with a priority. Elements with higher priority are dequeued before those with lower priority, regardless of their position in the queue.

Example of Priority Queue Application:

Job Scheduling: In an operating system, high-priority tasks are processed before low-priority ones.

4.7 Applications of Queues

Queues have numerous applications in both software and real-world systems:

Task scheduling: Queues manage tasks to be executed in order of arrival.
CPU scheduling: Used in process scheduling, particularly for handling multiple processes.
Breadth-First Search (BFS): In graph traversal algorithms, queues store nodes to be explored.
Resource sharing: Queues are used to manage shared resources like printers or database access.

4.8 Round Robin Scheduling

In Round Robin Scheduling, a queue is used to manage processes, each of which gets an equal time slice. After its time slice expires, the process is moved to the rear of the queue if it's not completed. This scheduling algorithm ensures fairness in resource allocation.

4.9 Job Scheduling using Queues

Job scheduling often uses queues to manage the execution of jobs in a system. Jobs are placed in a queue and executed in the order they arrive, or according to their priority if a priority queue is used.

4.10 Glossary

Queue: A linear Data Structure that follows FIFO (First In, First Out).
Enqueue: Operation to add an element to the rear of the queue.
Dequeue: Operation to remove an element from the front of the queue.
Circular Queue: A queue in which the rear wraps around to the front when the array becomes full.
Dequeue: A double-ended queue where elements can be added or removed from both ends.
Priority Queue: A queue where each element is associated with a priority, and higher-priority elements are processed first.

4.11 Summary

Queue: A linear Data Structure that follows First In, First Out (FIFO).
Core Operations:
- **Enqueue**: Adds an element to the rear of the queue.
- **Dequeue**: Removes an element from the front of the queue.
- **Peek**: Retrieves the front element without removing it.
- **IsEmpty**: Checks if the queue is empty.

Queue Implementations:
- **Array-based**: Fixed-size queue using arrays.
- **Linked list-based**: Dynamic queue using linked lists.

Circular Queue: A queue where the rear wraps around to the front when the array becomes full, solving space inefficiency.
Dequeue (Double-Ended Queue): Allows insertion and deletion from both front and rear ends.
Priority Queue: Processes elements based on priority rather than order of insertion.
Applications of Queues:
- **Task and CPU scheduling**.
- **Graph traversal** using Breadth-First Search (BFS).
- **Resource management** (e.g., printer or database access).

Round Robin Scheduling: Uses a queue to manage processes, giving each process equal time for execution.
Job Scheduling: Manages jobs in a queue for execution in order of arrival or priority.

4.12 Previous year Unsolved Questions

1. What is a Circular Queue? How does it differ from a queue? (IGNOU 2021)
2. Write an algorithm to enqueue and dequeue an element in a queue. (RTU 2023-24)
3. What is a Dequeue? How does it differ from a Queue? (IGNOU 2022)
4. Write a short note on Priority Queue. (MU 2021-22)
5. Explain the advantage of circular queue over linear queue. Write a function in C language to insert an element in circular queue. (MU 2021-22)

6. Define ''Queue''. Explain the operations that can be performed on a Queue. (IGNOU 2022)
7. Write a program to implement Circular queue using an array. (MU 2021-22)
8. Suppose a queue is implemented by a circular array QUEUE [0...9]. The number of elements in the queue, if FRONT = 8 and REAR = 3, will be (MU 2022-23)
   A.)3
   B.)4
   C.)5
   D.)6
9. How to define Queues using Array? What are limitations of singular queue? (Pune University 2019)
10. Give details explanation of Arry implementation of priority queue? What are applications of priority queue? (Pune University 2019)

Exercises

Exercise 1 – Multiple Choice Questions

1. Which of the following is true about a Queue?
   a) It is a LIFO structure
   b) It is a FIFO structure
   c) It stores elements in sorted order
   d) It allows access to elements randomly
2. What is the operation called when an element is added to the rear of a queue?
   a) Push
   b) Pop
   c) Enqueue
   d) Dequeue

Exercise 2 – True/False

1. In a circular queue, the last position is connected back to the first position.
2. A dequeue is a type of queue where elements can only be added at the rear.

Exercise 3 – Fill in the blanks

1. In a queue, the operation to add an element is called ______.
2. A______ queue allows insertion and deletion from both ends.

Exercise 4- Fill in the blanks with two options

1. In a queue, elements are added at the ______ and removed from the ______.
2. A ______ queue connects the last position back to the first, making it ______ in nature.

Exercise 5- Rearrange the sentence

1. In / a / and / queue / removed / the / elements / front / are / at / the / added / rear.
2. First / follows / a / FIFO / in / data / queue / structure.

Exercise 6- Choose the Odd One Out

1. Which one is the odd one out?
   A) Stack
   B) Circular Queue
   C) Deque
   D) Priority Queue
2. Which one is the odd one out?
   A) Stack
   B) Push
   C) Dequeue
   D) Front

Exercise 7- Jumble words

1. EEQUU
2. CEEUQNUE

Exercise 8- Match case

Column A

1. FIFO
2. Enqueue
3. Dequeue
4. Rear
5. Priority Queue

Column B
A. Circular Queue
b. Priority-based removal
c. Add an element to the queue
d. Remove an element from the queue
e. First In, First Out

Exercise 9- Assertion – Reason

1. **Assertion**: A queue is a linear Data Structure that follows the First-In-First-Out (FIFO) principle.
   Reason: In a queue, the last element added is the first to be removed.
   a) Both Assertion and Reason are correct explanation for Assertion.
   b) Both Assertion and Reason but Reason is the correct explanation for Assertion.
   c) Assertion is correct, but Reason is incorrect.
   d) Assertion is incorrect, but Reason is correct.

Exercise 10- Read the questions given below and find the appropriate word in the grid provided.

Q	W	E	R	T	Y	U	I	O
A	S	F	I	F	O	G	H	J
Z	X	C	Q	U	E	U	E	V
B	N	M	L	K	J	P	I	H
F	I	F	O	Q	W	E	D	F
O	I	U	E	R	Q	T	G	Z
M	P	K	J	Y	I	N	F	O

Find the following words in the grid:

1. Queue
2. FIFO

Exercise 11- One- word

1. What principle does a queue follow?
2. What operation is used to remove an element from the front of a queue?

Exercise 12- Small Answers

1. What is the difference between a stack and a queue?
2. Explain what a circular queue is.

Exercise 13- Long Answers

1. Explain the concept of a queue and its types in detail.
2. Describe the various operations performed in a queue and explain their time complexity.

Answers

Exercise 1-

1. b) It is a FIFO structure, 2. c) Enqueue

Exercise 2-

1. True, 2. False

Exercise 3-

1. Enqueue, 2. Deque

Exercise 4-

1. rear, front, 2. circular, cyclic

Exercise 5-

1. Elements are added at the rear and removed from the front in a queue.
2. A queue is a Data Structure that follows the FIFO principle.

Exercise 6-

1. a) Stack, 2. b) Push

Exercise 7-

1. Queue, 2. Enqueue

Exercise 8-

1-E,2-C,3-D,4-A,5-B

Exercise 9-

1. c) Assertion is correct, but Reason is incorrect.

Exercise 11-

1. FIFO, 2. Dequeue

Test Paper
Chapter-4
Queues

Time Duration: 30 Minutes **Maximum Marks: 25**

General Instructions:

1. The question paper consists of 12 questions and is divided into four sections, A, B, C and D.
2. All questions are compulsory.
3. Section A comprises MCQs, Fill in the blanks and True or False carrying one marks each.
4. Section B comprises VSAQs(very short answers questions) carrying two marks each.
5. Section C comprises SAQs(short questions) carrying four marks each.
6. Section D comprises long questions carrying five marks each.

SECTION-A

I. Multiple choice questions: **(1*2=2)**

1. Which of the following is NOT a type of queue?
   a) Simple queue
   b) Circular queue
   c) Priority queue
   d) Stack queue
2. What is the time complexity of inserting an element in a queue implemented using a linked list?
   a) O(1)
   b) O(n)
   c) O(log n)
   d) O(n log n)

II. Fill in the blanks: **(1*2=2)**

1. A ______ queue is where the last element is connected back to the first element to form a circle.
2. In a priority queue, elements are dequeued based on their ______.

III. True or False: **(1*2=2)**

1. In a queue, the front and rear pointers are always equal.
2. Queue follows the First-In-First-Out (FIFO) principle.

SECTION-B

IV. Very Short answers type questions-I **(2*3=6)**

1. Which Data Structure connects the rear end to the front end, forming a circle?
2. Which queue allows elements to be dequeued based on priority?
3. What is the term for adding an element to the rear of a queue?

SECTION-C

V. Short answers type questions-II **(4*2=8)**

1. What is the role of a rear pointer in a queue?
2. What is meant by the term 'underflow' in the context of queues?

SECTION-D

VI. Long answers type questions **(5*1=5)**

1. How is a circular queue implemented using an array? Explain the benefits of a circular queue over a simple queue.

Chapter 5 - Recursion and Applications

In this chapter you will learn about:
Introduction to Recursion
Writing Recursive Functions
Factorial Calculation using Recursion
Fibonacci Series using Recursion
Tower of Hanoi Problem using Recursion
Advantages and Limitations of Recursion
Recursion vs. Iteration

Recursion is a powerful programming technique where a function calls itself in order to solve smaller instances of the same problem. Recursion is commonly used for tasks that can be defined in terms of smaller subproblems, such as mathematical sequences, factorials, and algorithmic challenges like the Tower of Hanoi. This chapter covers the concept of recursion, how to write recursive functions, and explores various applications of recursion such as factorial calculation, Fibonacci series, and solving the Tower of Hanoi problem. We will also compare recursion with iteration and discuss the advantages and limitations of using recursion.

5.1 Introduction to Recursion

Recursion is a process in which a function calls itself as a part of its execution. A recursive function solves a problem by breaking it down into smaller subproblems of the same type. The two key elements in a recursive function are:

Base case: The condition under which the recursion terminates.

Recursive case: The part of the function where the recursion takes place, reducing the complexity of the problem.

For example, calculating the factorial of a number can be represented recursively as:

$$n! = n * (n-1)!$$

5.2 Writing Recursive Functions

When writing recursive functions, it is important to define both the base case and the recursive case. A well-structured recursive function must:

1. Define the base case to stop the recursion.
2. Call itself with a reduced problem size to approach the base case.

Example Program (Recursive Function to Calculate Factorial):

```
int factorial(int n) {
    if (n == 0) return 1;  // Base case
    else return n * factorial(n - 1);  // Recursive case
}
```

In this example, when n == 0, the recursion stops, and the function returns 1. Otherwise, the function calls itself with n-1 until it reaches the base case.

5.3 Factorial Calculation using Recursion

The factorial of a number n is the product of all integers from 1 to n. It can be calculated recursively as shown in the previous example. Factorial calculation is a classic problem for recursion, as the result of n! depends on (n-1)!.

Example:

5! = 5 * 4!
4! = 4 * 3!
3! = 3 * 2!
...
1! = 1 (Base case)

5.4 Fibonacci Series using Recursion

The Fibonacci series is another classic example of recursion. In this series, each number is the sum of the two preceding ones, starting from 0 and 1:

$$F(n) = F(n-1) + F(n-2), \text{ with } F(0) = 0, F(1) = 1$$

Example Program (Fibonacci Series using Recursion):

```
int fibonacci(int n) {
    if (n == 0) return 0;  // Base case
    if (n == 1) return 1;  // Base case
    return fibonacci(n - 1) + fibonacci(n - 2);  // Recursive case
}
```

5.5 Tower of Hanoi Problem using Recursion

The Tower of Hanoi is a well-known problem in computer science that involves moving a set of disks from one peg to another, following specific rules. The problem can be solved recursively by breaking it down into smaller subproblems:

1. **Move n-1 disks from the source peg to an auxiliary peg.**
2. **Move the nth disk to the target peg.**
3. **Move the n-1 disks from the auxiliary peg to the target peg.**

Example:
For n disks, the recursive solution involves moving n-1 disks and then solving for the last disk.

Example Program (Recursive Solution for Tower of Hanoi):

```
void towerOfHanoi(int n, char from_peg, char to_peg, char aux_peg) {
    if (n == 1) {
        printf("Move disk 1 from %c to %c\n", from_peg, to_peg);
        return;
    }
    towerOfHanoi(n - 1, from_peg, aux_peg, to_peg);
    printf("Move disk %d from %c to %c\n", n, from_peg, to_peg);
    towerOfHanoi(n - 1, aux_peg, to_peg, from_peg);
}
```

5.6 Advantages and Limitations of Recursion

Advantages:

Simplicity: Recursion simplifies the code for problems that have a recursive structure, such as factorials, Fibonacci numbers, and tree traversals.

Elegance: Recursive solutions are often more elegant and easier to understand when compared to iterative solutions for certain problems.

Limitations:

Performance: Recursive functions can lead to performance issues due to repeated function calls and increased memory usage (stack frames).

Risk of Stack Overflow: Recursion can lead to stack overflow if the base case is not properly defined or if the depth of recursion is too large.

5.7 Recursion vs. Iteration

Recursion: Solves a problem by reducing it into smaller instances of the same problem. It requires more memory due to the overhead of function calls.

Iteration: Uses looping constructs to repeat a set of operations. Iterative solutions are generally more memory-efficient and faster in execution.

Comparison Table:

Aspect	Recursion	Iteration
Memory	Requires more memory (stack)	Requires less memory
Speed	Can be slower due to function calls	Generally faster
Complexity	Easier to implement for recursive problems	Requires more lines of code for complex problems
Examples	Factorial, Fibonacci, Tower of Hanoi	Loops, Arrays

5.8 Glossary

Recursion: A process where a function calls itself.
Base Case: The condition under which the recursion terminates.
Recursive Case: The part of a recursive function where it calls itself to break the problem down.
Stack Overflow: An error that occurs when too many recursive calls consume all available memory.

5.9 Summary

Recursion: A function that calls itself to solve a smaller instance of the same problem.
Base Case: The condition under which the recursion stops.
Recursive Case: The part of the function where it calls itself with a reduced problem size.
Factorial Calculation: Recursion is used to calculate factorials, breaking down the problem into n * (n-1)!.
Fibonacci Series: Fibonacci numbers are computed using recursion where each term is the sum of the two preceding ones.
Tower of Hanoi: Solving the disk-moving problem using recursion by breaking it down into smaller moves.
Advantages: Simplifies complex problems, provides elegant solutions for recursive problems like tree traversal.
Limitations: Can lead to performance issues (stack overflow and increased memory usage).
Recursion vs. Iteration: Recursion uses more memory due to function calls, while iteration is more efficient but may require more complex code.
Applications: Useful in divide-and-conquer algorithms, tree/graph traversals, and problems that have a recursive nature.

5.10 Previous year Unsolved Questions

1. (a) What is Breadth First Search? How does it differ from Depth First Search? (IGNOU-2022)
   (b) What is Hashing? Write a short note on it.
2. What is meant by Minimum Cost Spanning Tree (MCST)? How can you find it? (IGNOU-2022)
3. A node of a B-Tree has 1 key values. How many children for this nod possible? (RTU 2023-24)
4. Write algorithm to obtain Minimum Cost Spanning tree for a given graph. Explain through example of a graph containing 7 vertices and compute cost of the tree. (RTU 2023-24)
5. What is a MST? Differentiate between Kruskal and Prim's algorithm with their time complexity. (RTU 2023-24)
6. Write a recursive program for towers of Hanoi. (RTU 2023-24)
7. ____________________ is used in implementation of recursion. (MU 2022-23)
8. How sentinel search algorithm works? Discuss the limitations of linear search? (Pune University 2019)

Exercises

Exercise 1 – Multiple Choice Questions

1. What is recursion?
   a) A function that calls itself
   b) A function that repeats indefinitely
   c) A loop inside a function
   d) A function that only accepts integers
2. Which of the following is necessary for a recursive function to avoid infinite recursion?
   a) Return statement
   b) Recursive call
   c) Base case
   d) Loop

Exercise 2 – True/False

1. Recursion must always have a base case to prevent infinite loops.
2. Recursive functions always consume less memory than iterative functions.

Exercise 3 – Fill in the blanks

1. The function calls itself in recursion until a ______ is met.
2. Recursion often uses more ______ because of the need to maintain multiple function calls on the call stack.

Exercise 4- Fill in the blanks with two options

1. In recursion, the function calls itself until it reaches a ______ case, and the recursive calls are stored in the ______.
2. A ______ recursion occurs when the recursive call is the last statement, and it can be optimized by some compilers to reduce the ______ overhead.

Exercise 5- Rearrange the sentence

1. Base / a / recursion / function / must / terminate / case / with.
2. Problems / recursion / can / divide / complex / simpler / into.

Exercise 6- Choose the Odd One Out

1. Which one is the odd one out?
   A) Factorial calculation
   B) Fibonacci sequence
   C) Binary search
   D) Bubble sort
2. Which one is the odd one out?
   A) Base case
   B) Recursive call
   C) Loop condition
   D) Stack memory

Exercise 7- Jumble words

1. VSAAERIOTN ERCUSRIOR
2. SSBEEA CLAL

Exercise 8- Match case

Column A

1. Base Case
2. Recursion
3. Tail Recursion
4. Fibonacci Sequence

5. Call Stack

Column B
A. Last operation in a recursive call
B. Uses First-In-Last-Out (FILO) order
C. Condition to terminate recursion
D. A function calls itself
E. Classic problem solved using recursion

Exercise 9- Assertion – Reason

1. **Assertion:** Recursion can solve problems by breaking them into smaller sub-problems.
Reason: Recursion helps in reducing memory usage by eliminating the need for loops.
a) Both Assertion and Reason are correct explanation for Assertion.
b) Both Assertion and Reason but Reason is the correct explanation for Assertion.
c) Assertion is correct, but Reason is incorrect.
d) Assertion is incorrect, but Reason is correct.

Exercise 10- Read the questions given below and find the appropriate word in the grid provided.

R	E	C	U	R	S	I	O	N
A	G	T	Y	O	W	P	Q	R
C	N	L	U	P	M	F	H	Z
T	F	A	C	T	O	R	I	A
O	Y	B	D	E	F	U	G	L
R	I	A	C	H	J	V	A	X
I	A	Z	K	S	T	T	W	M
A	L	W	N	X	E	K	I	L

Find the following words in the grid:
1. Recursion
2. Factorial

Exercise 11- One- word

1. What is the term for a condition that stops recursion?
2. What type of recursion occurs when the recursive call is the last operation in the function?

Exercise 12- Small Answers

1. What is recursion and how does it work?
2. What is the difference between direct and indirect recursion?

Exercise 13- Long Answers

1. Explain the concept of recursion with an example. Discuss the advantages and disadvantages of using recursion in programming.
2. Explain the concept of tail recursion and how it can be optimized. Provide an example of a tail-recursive function and explain its
advantage over non-tail recursion.

Answers

Exercise 1-

1. a) A function that calls itself, 2. c) Base case

Exercise 2-

1. True, 2. False

Exercise 3-

1. base case, 2. memory

Exercise 4-

1. base, call stack, 2. tail, stack

Exercise 5-

1. A recursion function must terminate with a base case, 2. Recursion can divide complex problems into simpler ones.

Exercise 6-

1. d) Bubble sort, 2. c) Loop condition

Exercise 7-

1. Recursion vs Iteration, 2. Base Case

Exercise 8-

1-C,2-D,3-A,4-E,5-B

Exercise 9-

1. c) Assertion is correct, but Reason is incorrect.

Exercise 11-

1. Base case, 2. Tail recursion

Test Paper

Chapter-5
Recursion and Applications

Time Duration: 30 Minutes **Maximum Marks: 25**

General Instructions:

1. The question paper consists of 12 questions and is divided into four sections, A, B, C and D.
2. All questions are compulsory.
3. Section A comprises MCQs, Fill in the blanks and True or False carrying one marks each.
4. Section B comprises VSAQs(very short answers questions) carrying two marks each.
5. Section C comprises SAQs(short questions) carrying four marks each.
6. Section D comprises long questions carrying five marks each.

SECTION-A

I. Multiple choice questions: **(1*2=2)**

1. What is the typical advantage of recursion over iteration?
   a) Faster performance
   b) Simpler and cleaner code
   c) Uses less memory
   d) No advantage
2. In which problem-solving method is recursion most commonly used?
   a) Divide and conquer
   b) Greedy algorithms
   c) Dynamic programming
   d) Backtracking

II. Fill in the blanks: **(1*2=2)**

1. A recursive function that does not have a base case will result in an ________.
2. In tail recursion, the recursive call is the ______ operation performed in the function.

III. True or False: **(1*2=2)**

1. Recursion can be replaced by iteration in any scenario.
2. Recursion is generally more efficient than iteration.

SECTION-B

IV. Very Short answers type questions-I **(2*3=6)**

1. Which Data Structure is used to store recursive function calls?
2. Which famous mathematical sequence is commonly solved using recursion?
3. What principle does recursion rely on to solve problems?

SECTION-C

V. Short answers type questions-II **(4*2=8)**

1. What is the base case in recursion, and why is it important?
2. How does recursion relate to the divide and conquer approach?

SECTION-D

VI. Long answers type questions **(5*1=5)**

1. Discuss the difference between recursion and iteration. When should recursion be preferred over iteration, and vice versa?

Chapter 6 - Sorting Techniques

In this chapter you will learn about:

Introduction to Sorting
Bubble Sort
Selection Sort
Insertion Sort
Quick Sort
Merge Sort
Heap Sort
Radix Sort
Counting Sort
Shell Sort
Stability in Sorting Algorithms

Sorting is one of the most fundamental operations in computer science. It involves arranging data in a specific order, typically either ascending or descending. Sorting algorithms are crucial for tasks like searching, data organization, and optimization. There are numerous sorting techniques, each with its own advantages, complexities, and use cases. This chapter introduces the concept of sorting, followed by an exploration of key sorting algorithms like Bubble Sort, Selection Sort, Quick Sort, Merge Sort, and others, along with their algorithmic explanations, time complexities, and real-world applications. Diagrams, code examples, and performance analysis are provided to enhance understanding.

6.1 Introduction to Sorting

Sorting organizes elements in a list into a specific order. The two most common types of sorting orders are:

- **Ascending Order**: Smallest to largest (e.g., 1, 2, 3, 4...).
- **Descending Order**: Largest to smallest (e.g., 9, 8, 7, 6...).

Sorting is essential because it improves the efficiency of searching algorithms and makes data more readable and usable. Sorting algorithms can be classified based on:

- **Time Complexity**: How fast the algorithm runs (e.g., O(n^2), O(n log n)).
- **Space Complexity**: The amount of memory used.
- **Stability**: Whether the relative order of equal elements is preserved.

6.2 Bubble Sort: Algorithm and Analysis

Bubble Sort repeatedly compares adjacent elements and swaps them if they are in the wrong order. This process continues until no swaps are required.

Algorithm:

1. Traverse the array.
2. Compare adjacent elements and swap if needed.
3. Repeat the process until the array is sorted.

Example Program:

```
void bubbleSort(int arr[], int n) {
  for (int i = 0; i < n-1; i++) {
    for (int j = 0; j < n-i-1; j++) {
      if (arr[j] > arr[j+1]) {
        int temp = arr[j];
        arr[j] = arr[j+1];
        arr[j+1] = temp;
      }
    }
  }
}
```

Time Complexity: O(n^2)
Space Complexity: O(1)
Stability: Stable

6.3 Selection Sort: Algorithm and Analysis

Selection Sort selects the minimum element from the unsorted part of the array and swaps it with the first unsorted element.

Algorithm:

1. Traverse the array to find the minimum element.
2. Swap it with the first unsorted element.
3. Move the boundary between the sorted and unsorted portions of the array.

Time Complexity: O(n^2)
Space Complexity: O(1)
Stability: Not stable

6.4 Insertion Sort: Algorithm and Analysis

Insertion Sort builds the sorted array one element at a time by repeatedly inserting unsorted elements into their correct position.

Algorithm:

1. Start from the second element.
2. Compare it with previous elements and shift larger elements one position to the right.
3. Insert the element in its correct position.

Time Complexity: O(n^2)
Space Complexity: O(1)
Stability: Stable

6.5 Quick Sort: Algorithm and Analysis

Quick Sort is a divide-and-conquer algorithm that partitions the array into two parts: one with smaller elements and one with larger elements. It recursively sorts both parts.

Algorithm:

1. Choose a pivot element.
2. Partition the array so that elements less than the pivot are on one side and those greater are on the other.
3. Recursively apply quicksort to both subarrays.

Time Complexity: O(n log n) on average, O(n^2) in the worst case
Space Complexity: O(log n)
Stability: Not stable

6.6 Merge Sort: Algorithm and Analysis

Merge Sort is another divide-and-conquer algorithm. It recursively divides the array into two halves, sorts them, and then merges the sorted halves.

Algorithm:

1. Recursively split the array into two halves.
2. Sort both halves.
3. Merge the two sorted halves back together.

Time Complexity: O(n log n)
Space Complexity: O(n)
Stability: Stable

6.7 Heap Sort: Algorithm and Analysis

Heap Sort transforms the array into a binary heap (max heap or min heap) and repeatedly extracts the root element to build the sorted array.

Algorithm:

1. Build a max heap from the input array.
2. Extract the root (maximum element), place it at the end of the array, and reduce the heap size.

3. Heapify the remaining elements.

Time Complexity: O(n log n)
Space Complexity: O(1)
Stability: Not stable

6.8 Radix Sort: Algorithm and Analysis

Radix Sort sorts numbers digit by digit, starting from the least significant digit to the most significant digit. It uses a stable counting sort as a subroutine.

Algorithm:

1. Perform counting sort for each digit, starting with the least significant digit.
2. Repeat the process until all digits are sorted.

Time Complexity: O(d(n + k)) where d is the number of digits and k is the range of digits
Space Complexity: O(n + k)
Stability: Stable

6.9 Counting Sort: Algorithm and Analysis

Counting Sort works by counting the number of occurrences of each distinct element and then using that count to place elements in their correct position.

Algorithm:

1. Count occurrences of each element.
2. Modify the count array to reflect the position of each element.
3. Place elements in their sorted positions based on the count array.

Time Complexity: O(n + k)
Space Complexity: O(n + k)
Stability: Stable

6.10 Shell Sort: Algorithm and Analysis

Shell Sort is a variation of insertion sort that allows the exchange of far-apart elements, reducing the overall number of swaps.

Algorithm:

1. Divide the array into subarrays based on a gap sequence.
2. Sort each subarray using insertion sort.
3. Reduce the gap and repeat until the gap is 1.

Time Complexity: O(n^3/2)
Space Complexity: O(1)
Stability: Not stable

6.11 Stability in Sorting Algorithms

A stable sorting algorithm preserves the relative order of elements with equal keys. Stability is important in scenarios where secondary sorting criteria are involved. For example, in sorting employee records by age, if two employees have the same age, their order should be preserved according to their initial position.

Stable Sorting Algorithms: Merge Sort, Bubble Sort, Insertion Sort, Counting Sort, Radix Sort
Non-Stable Sorting Algorithms: Quick Sort, Heap Sort, Selection Sort, Shell Sort

6.12 Glossary

Stable Sorting: Sorting that preserves the relative order of equal elements.
Time Complexity: The measure of the number of operations an algorithm performs.
Space Complexity: The measure of memory used by an algorithm.
In-Place Sorting: A sorting algorithm that uses a constant amount of extra space.

6.13 Summary

Sorting: The process of arranging data in a specific order (ascending/descending).
Bubble Sort: Repeatedly compares and swaps adjacent elements; time complexity O(n^2); stable.

Selection Sort: Selects the minimum element and swaps it with the current element; time complexity $O(n^2)$; not stable.
Insertion Sort: Builds a sorted array one element at a time by inserting elements into their correct position; time complexity $O(n^2)$; stable.
Quick Sort: A divide-and-conquer algorithm that partitions the array; average time complexity $O(n \log n)$; not stable.
Merge Sort: Recursively divides and merges the array; time complexity $O(n \log n)$; stable.
Heap Sort: Builds a binary heap and repeatedly extracts the maximum element; time complexity $O(n \log n)$; not stable.
Radix Sort: Sorts numbers digit by digit using a stable counting sort; time complexity $O(d(n + k))$; stable.
Counting Sort: Counts occurrences and places elements accordingly; time complexity $O(n + k)$; stable.
Shell Sort: A variation of insertion sort using a gap sequence; time complexity O(n^3/2); not stable.
Stability: Preserving the relative order of equal elements is crucial for certain use cases.

6.14 Previous year Unsolved Questions

1. Write an algorithm for bubble sort. Sort the following set of data in ascending order using bubble sort. Show all steps of application of algorithm: 100, 50, 60, 70, 150, 80 (IGNOU 2021)
2. Sort the following elements using quick sort: (RTU 2023-24)
   28 5 16 36 11 19 25
3. Show the result of sorting the following numbers using insertion sort (step by step o/p) (RTU 2023-24)
   4, 7, 3, 2, 5, 1, 6
4. What is Breadth First Search? How does it differ from Depth First Search? (IGNOU 2022)
5. How does the Quicksort technique work? Give C function for the same. (MU 2023-24)
6. What is Linear Search? How does it differ from Binary Search? (IGNOU 2022)
7. Compare Bubble sort, Insertion sort and Selection sort techniques. (Pune University 2019)
8. Write Quick sort algorithm and explain with example. (Pune University 2019)

Exercises

Exercise 1 – Multiple Choice Questions

1. What is the height of a tree?
   a) The number of leaves in the tree
   b) The number of nodes in the tree
   c) The number of edges from the root to the deepest leaf
   d) The number of edges in the longest path from any node to a leaf
2. Which of the following is true for a binary tree?
   a) Each node has at most two children
   b) Each node has exactly two children
   c) The tree is always balanced
   d) There is no specific rule for children of a node

Exercise 2 – True/False

1. In a binary tree, a node can have more than two children.
2. A complete binary tree is a binary tree in which all the levels are completely filled except possibly the last one.

Exercise 3 – Fill in the blanks

1. In a binary tree, each node has at most _______ children.
2. The height of a tree is the number of _______ on the longest path from the root to a leaf.

Exercise 4- Fill in the blanks with two options

1. In a binary search tree, the left subtree contains nodes with values _______ than the root, while the right subtree contains nodes with values _______ than the root.
2. The height of a complete binary tree with 'n' nodes is _______ and it contains _______ leaves in its last level.

Exercise 5- Rearrange the sentence

1. The / tree / traversal / visits / level / nodes / order / in / a.
2. Root / the / in / has / tree / no / node / parent / a.

Exercise 6- Choose the Odd One Out

1. Which one is the odd one out?
   A) In-order
   B) Pre-order
   C) Post-order
   D) Level-order
2. Which one is the odd one out?
   A) Binary Tree
   B) AVL Tree
   C) Red-Black Tree
   D) Stack

Exercise 7- Jumble words

1. EELRV-REDOR
2. BINRAY-RATHCSE-TEEER

Exercise 8- Match case

Column A
1. Binary Tree
2. AVL Tree

3. Leaf Node
4. Root Node
5. Height of Tree

Column B
A) A node that has no children
B) A tree in which each node has at most two children
C) A self-balancing binary search tree
D) The number of edges from the root to the deepest leaf
E) The topmost node in a tree

Exercise 9- Assertion – Reason

1. **Assertion:** A binary search tree ensures efficient searching, insertion, and deletion operations.
   Reason: A binary search tree is always balanced.
   a) Both Assertion and Reason are correct explanation for Assertion.
   b) Both Assertion and Reason but Reason is the correct explanation for Assertion.
   c) Assertion is correct, but Reason is incorrect.
   d) Assertion is incorrect, but Reason is correct.

Exercise 10- Read the questions given below and find the appropriate word in the grid provided.

B	U	B	B	L	E	N	Q	P
H	M	E	R	G	E	O	L	K
X	W	P	O	I	Y	R	J	Z
N	V	G	H	I	P	E	S	T
C	A	M	Q	L	B	E	F	U
F	D	R	P	L	A	E	U	Y
L	M	Z	G	K	I	L	Q	V

Find the following words in the grid:

1. Bubble
2. Merge

Exercise 11- One- word

1. What is the topmost node in a tree called?
2. What is a node with no children called?

Exercise 12- Small Answers

1. What is a Binary Search Tree (BST)?
2. What is the difference between a complete binary tree and a full binary tree?

Exercise 13- Long Answers

1. Explain the different types of tree traversal techniques with examples.
2. What are the properties of a Binary Search Tree (BST)? Explain how insertion and deletion work in a BST.

Answers

Exercise 1-

1. c) The number of edges from the root to the deepest leaf, 2. a) Each node has at most two children

Exercise 2-

1. False, 2. True

Exercise 3-

1. Two, 2. edges

Exercise 4-

1. smaller, larger, 2. log(n), n/2

Exercise 5-

1. A level-order traversal visits nodes in the tree., 2. The root node in a tree has no parent.

Exercise 6-

1. Depth-first search (DFS), 2. Stack

Exercise 7-

1. Level-order, 2. Binary Search Tree

Exercise 8-

1-B,2-C,3-A,4-E,5-D

Exercise 9-

1. c) Assertion is correct, but Reason is incorrect.

Exercise 11-

1. Root, 2. Leaf

Test Paper

Chapter-6
Sorting Techniques

Time Duration: 30 Minutes **Maximum Marks: 25**

General Instructions:
1. The question paper consists of 12 questions and is divided into four sections, A, B, C and D.
2. All questions are compulsory.
3. Section A comprises MCQs, Fill in the blanks and True or False carrying one marks each.
4. Section B comprises VSAQs(very short answers questions) carrying two marks each.
5. Section C comprises SAQs(short questions) carrying four marks each.
6. Section D comprises long questions carrying five marks each.

SECTION-A

I. Multiple choice questions: **(1*2=2)**

1. What is a full binary tree?
   a) A tree where each node has 0 or 2 children
   b) A tree where each node has exactly one child
   c) A tree where all nodes are of the same level
   d) A tree where all leaves are at the same level
2. In a Binary Search Tree (BST), which of the following is true?
   a) Left subtree contains only nodes with values smaller than the root
   b) Right subtree contains only nodes with values smaller than the root
   c) Both subtrees can have any values
   d) Left subtree contains only nodes with values larger than the root

II. Fill in the blanks: **(1*2=2)**

1. A binary search tree (BST) is a tree Data Structure where the left subtree contains only nodes with values _______ than the root.
2. A ______ traversal visits nodes of a tree level by level.

III. True or False: **(1*2=2)**

1. In an AVL tree, the difference between the heights of the left and right subtrees for every node can be more than 1.
2. A binary search tree allows duplicate elements.

SECTION-B

IV. Very Short answers type questions-I **(2*3=6)**

1. What type of traversal visits nodes level by level?
2. Which tree is a self-balancing binary search tree?
3. What is the maximum number of children a node in a binary tree can have?

SECTION-C

V. Short answers type questions-II **(4*2=8)**

1. Explain the concept of tree height.
2. What is the purpose of an AVL tree?

SECTION-D

VI. Long answers type questions **(5*1=5)**

1. What is an AVL tree? Explain how balancing is maintained in an AVL tree and why it is important.

Chapter 7 - Searching Techniques

In this chapter you will learn about:

Introduction to Searching
Linear Search
Binary Search
Fibonacci Search
Index Sequential Search
Applications of Searching in Data Structures

Searching is one of the fundamental operations in computer science, where the goal is to find the location of a specific element within a collection of data. Whether it's locating a record in a database or searching for a specific key in a large dataset, efficient searching algorithms are vital for performance optimization. This chapter introduces basic and advanced searching techniques, including Linear Search, Binary Search, Fibonacci Search, and Index Sequential Search. The efficiency and complexity of each algorithm are analyzed, along with practical applications and examples.

7.1 Introduction to Searching

Searching refers to the process of finding the location of a target element (key) within a collection, such as an array or list. The efficiency of searching algorithms can drastically affect the performance of software, especially when dealing with large datasets. Searching algorithms are generally categorized into two types:

Sequential Searching: Each element is checked in sequence until the target is found.

Divide and Conquer Searching: The search space is repeatedly divided in half to locate the target.

7.2 Linear Search: Algorithm and Analysis

Linear Search is the simplest search algorithm, where each element of the array or list is checked sequentially until the target element is found or the entire collection is traversed.

Algorithm:

1. Start from the first element.
2. Compare the target element with each element of the list.
3. If the target matches, return its position.
4. If not, continue until the end of the list.

Example Program:

```
int linearSearch(int arr[], int n, int key) {
  for (int i = 0; i < n; i++) {
    if (arr[i] == key) {
      return i;  // Target found
    }
  }
  return -1;  // Target not found
}
```

Time Complexity: O(n)
Space Complexity: O(1)
Best Used When: The dataset is small or unsorted.

7.3 Binary Search: Algorithm and Analysis

Binary Search is a highly efficient search algorithm that works only on sorted datasets. It uses a divide-and-conquer approach by repeatedly halving the search space.

Algorithm:

1. Start with the middle element of the sorted list.
2. If the middle element is the target, return its index.
3. If the target is smaller than the middle element, repeat the process on the left half.
4. If the target is larger, repeat the process on the right half.

Example Program:

```
int binarySearch(int arr[], int low, int high, int key) {
  while (low <= high) {
    int mid = (low + high) / 2;
    if (arr[mid] == key)
      return mid;
    else if (arr[mid] < key)
      low = mid + 1;
    else
      high = mid - 1;
  }
  return -1; // Target not found
}
```

Time Complexity: O(log n)
Space Complexity: O(1)
Best Used When: The dataset is large and sorted.

7.4 Fibonacci Search: Algorithm and Analysis

Fibonacci Search is another divide-and-conquer search algorithm that uses Fibonacci numbers to divide the array into smaller subarrays. Like Binary Search, it works only on sorted arrays.

Algorithm:

1. Determine the smallest Fibonacci number that is greater than or equal to the size of the array.
2. Use the Fibonacci numbers to divide the search space and perform comparisons.
3. Continue dividing the subarrays based on Fibonacci numbers until the target element is found.

Time Complexity: O(log n)
Space Complexity: O(1)
Best Used When: Suitable for large sorted datasets, especially when the division is better suited to Fibonacci sequence properties.

7.5 Index Sequential Search: Concepts and Applications

Index Sequential Search is a combination of sequential and binary search. An index is built on top of the data to divide it into blocks, allowing quick jumps between sections of the data, followed by a sequential search within each block.

Process:

1. Build an index to divide the array into blocks.
2. Use the index to quickly locate the block that might contain the target.
3. Perform a linear search within the block.

Time Complexity: O(n) in the worst case, but faster with efficient indexing
Best Used When: Suitable for large datasets where index creation is practical.

7.6 Applications of Searching in Data Structures

Searching techniques are used across many different Data Structures:

Arrays and Lists: Basic searching algorithms like Linear Search and Binary Search are applied here.
Trees: Searching for nodes within binary search trees (BSTs) and balanced trees (AVL trees).
Graphs: Graph traversal techniques like Breadth-First Search (BFS) and Depth-First Search (DFS) are forms of searching.

Key applications include:

Database Querying: Searching through records efficiently.
Data Retrieval: Retrieving files from memory or storage.
Routing Algorithms: Finding the shortest path in network and graph problems.

7.7 Glossary

Search Space: The range or section of data being searched.

Sequential Search: Searching each element one by one.
Divide and Conquer: A strategy that divides the search space into smaller subproblems.
Indexing: Creating an additional structure that allows faster access to data.
Fibonacci Search: A divide-and-conquer method based on Fibonacci numbers.

7.8 Summary

Searching: The process of finding the location of a specific element in a dataset.
Linear Search: Sequentially checks each element until the target is found; time complexity O(n); best for small, unsorted datasets.
Binary Search: Efficient, divide-and-conquer search for sorted datasets; time complexity O(log n).
Fibonacci Search: Similar to binary search but uses Fibonacci numbers to divide the search space; time complexity O(log n); suited for large sorted datasets.
Index Sequential Search: Combines sequential and binary search using an index to quickly find data in large collections.
Applications: Searching algorithms are used in arrays, trees, graphs, databases, and network routing.
Efficiency: Algorithms like Binary and Fibonacci Search are optimal for sorted and large datasets, while Linear Search is simpler for smaller, unsorted lists.

7.9 Previous year Unsolved Questions

1. What is Binary Search? Explain it with an example. (IGNOU 2021)
2. Illustrate different traversal techniques used in binary search trees. (RTU 2023-24)
3. A node of a B-Tree has 1 key values. How many children for this nod possible? (RTU 2023-24)
4. What is Linear Search? How does it differ from Binary Search? (IGNOU 2022)
5. Describe the structure of a threaded binary tree through example. (RTU 2023-24)
6. Write algorithm to obtain Minimum Cost Spanning tree for a given graph. Explain through example of a graph containing 7 vertices and compute cost of the tree. (RTU 2023-24)
8. Examine the relationship between number of nodes and height of AVL tree. (RTU 2023-24)
9. What is Breadth First Search? How does it differ from Depth First Search? (IGNOU 2022)
10. Applying binary search on following data and show step by step working 3, 7, 11, 15, 23, 34, 47, 49, 59, 63, 64, 70, 86, 90. To search key 15 in it. (Pune University 2019)

Exercises

Exercise 1 – Multiple Choice Questions

1. What is the time complexity of performing Breadth-First Search (BFS) on a graph with V vertices and E edges?
   a) O(V + E)
   b) O(V^2)
   c) O(E^2)
   d) O(V * E)
2. Which of the following is an application of Depth-First Search (DFS)?
   a) Detecting cycles in a graph
   b) Finding the shortest path in a weighted graph
   c) Sorting a list of numbers
   d) Balancing a binary tree

Exercise 2 – True/False

1. In a directed graph, the in-degree of a node is the number of edges coming into the node.
2. A graph with no cycles is called a cyclic graph.

Exercise 3 – Fill in the blanks

1. In a graph, the shortest path between two nodes can be found using _______ algorithm.
2. The degree of a node in an undirected graph is the number of _______ incident to it.

Exercise 4- Fill in the blanks with two options

1. In an undirected graph, the sum of the degrees of all vertices is equal to _______ times the number of _______.
2. In Depth-First Search (DFS), nodes are explored as deeply as possible before _______ and returning to explore the _______ nodes.

Exercise 5- Rearrange the sentence

1. Path / the / shortest / between / algorithm / finds / two / vertices / Dijkstra's.
2. Vertices / the / is / node / between / degree / number / of / edges / a / and other.

Exercise 6- Choose the Odd One Out

1. Which one is the odd one out?
   A) Breadth-First Search
   B) Depth-First Search
   C) Kruskal's Algorithm
   D) Insertion Sort

2. Which one is the odd one out?
   A) Adjacency Matrix
   B) Stack
   C) Queue
   D) Linked List

Exercise 7- Jumble words

1. LTGAIRHO-MARHTIX
2. SPEHTD-RITFS-SRAHEC

Exercise 8- Match case

Column A

1. Adjacency Matrix
2. Breadth-First Search

3. Depth-First Search
4. Spanning Tree
5. Cycle

Column B
A) A list where each vertex has a list of adjacent vertices
B) An algorithm that explores the graph level by level
C) A matrix used to represent graph edges with a 2D array
D) A tree that covers all vertices of a graph with the minimum number of edges
E) A path in a graph that starts and ends at the same vertex

Exercise 9- Assertion – Reason

1. Assertion: An adjacency list is more space-efficient than an adjacency matrix for representing sparse graphs.
Reason: In an adjacency list, only the edges are stored, whereas an adjacency matrix stores every possible edge between nodes, including non-existent ones.

a) Both Assertion and Reason are correct explanation for Assertion.
b) Both Assertion and Reason but Reason is the correct explanation for Assertion.
c) Assertion is correct, but Reason is incorrect.
d) Assertion is incorrect, but Reason is correct.

Exercise 10- Read the questions given below and find the appropriate word in the grid provided.

B	I	N	A	R	Y	T	R	L
X	M	L	P	S	R	E	H	Q
C	T	I	N	E	A	R	G	J
F	P	E	L	I	D	F	U	W
M	K	A	O	Q	N	Y	B	X
L	B	I	N	U	Q	R	W	Z
E	A	V	Z	X	Y	I	T	E

Find the following words in the grid:

1. Binary
2. Linear

Exercise 11- One- word

1. What is the Data Structure used to implement Breadth-First Search (BFS)?
2. What is the minimum number of edges required to connect all vertices in a graph called?

Exercise 12- Small Answers

1. What is the difference between a directed and undirected graph?
2. Explain what a cycle in a graph is.

Exercise 13- Long Answers

1. Explain the differences between Depth-First Search (DFS) and Breadth-First Search (BFS) in graphs. Provide an example for each.
2. What is a minimum spanning tree (MST)? Explain the working of Kruskal's algorithm with an example.

Answers

Exercise 1-

1. a) O (V + E), 2. a) Detecting cycles in a graph

Exercise 2-

1. True, 2. False

Exercise 3-

1. Dijkstra's, 2. edges

Exercise 4-

1. 2, edges, 2. backtracking, unvisited

Exercise 5-

1. Dijkstra's algorithm finds the shortest path between two vertices, 2. The degree of a node is the number of edges between the node and other vertices.

Exercise 6-

1. Insertion Sort, 2. Adjacency Matrix

Exercise 7-

1. Adjacency Matrix, 2. Depth-First Search

Exercise 8-

1-C,2-B,3-A,4-D,5-E

Exercise 9-

1. b) Both Assertion and Reason but Reason is the correct explanation for Assertion.

Exercise 11-

1. Queue, 2. Spanning Tree

Test Paper

Chapter-7
Searching Techniques

Time Duration: 30 Minutes **Maximum Marks: 25**

General Instructions:
1. The question paper consists of 12 questions and is divided into four sections, A, B, C and D.
2. All questions are compulsory.
3. Section A comprises MCQs, Fill in the blanks and True or False carrying one marks each.
4. Section B comprises VSAQs(very short answers questions) carrying two marks each.
5. Section C comprises SAQs(short questions) carrying four marks each.
6. Section D comprises long questions carrying five marks each.

SECTION-A

I. Multiple choice questions: **(1*2=2)**

1. Which Data Structure is typically used to implement Depth-First Search (DFS)?
   a) Queue
   b) Stack
   c) Heap
   d) Priority Queue
2. In an undirected graph, what is the degree of a node?
   a) The number of edges incident to the node
   b) The number of connected components
   c) The shortest path to the root node
   d) The total number of nodes in the graph

II. Fill in the blanks: **(1*2=2)**

1. A graph with no cycles is called a _______ graph.
2. In a directed graph, the total number of incoming edges to a node is called its _______.

III. True or False: **(1*2=2)**

1. An adjacency matrix requires more space than an adjacency list to represent sparse graphs.
2. In a complete graph, there are no edges between the vertices.

SECTION-B

IV. Very Short answers type questions-I **(2*3=6)**

1. What type of graph contains no cycles?
2. What is the representation of a graph using a 2D array called?
3. Which algorithm is used to find the shortest path in a weighted graph?

SECTION-C

V. Short answers type questions-II **(4*2=8)**

1. What is the adjacency list representation of a graph?
2. What is a connected graph?

SECTION-D

VI. Long answers type questions **(5*1=5)**

1. Explain the adjacency matrix and adjacency list representations of graphs. What are the advantages and disadvantages of each?

Chapter 8 - Tree

In this chapter you will learn about:

Basic Tree Concepts and Terminology
Binary Trees
Binary Tree Traversals
Binary Search Trees
Advanced Trees
Threaded Binary Trees
Applications of Trees

Trees are hierarchical Data Structures that represent a collection of nodes connected by edges. Unlike linear Data Structures such as arrays and linked lists, trees are used to represent hierarchical relationships, such as organizational structures, file systems, and decision-making processes. In computer science, trees are essential for search algorithms, sorting, and data storage. This chapter delves into the basic concepts of trees, binary trees, traversals, advanced trees like AVL and B-Trees, and various applications of trees in computing. Diagrams, programs, and examples are included for a clearer understanding of these structures.

8.1 Basic Tree Concepts and Terminology

A **tree** consists of nodes where each node contains data and possibly references to other nodes (children). The key terms associated with trees are:

- **Root**: The topmost node in a tree.
- **Node**: A point in the tree containing data and possibly children nodes.
- **Edge**: The connection between two nodes.
- **Leaf**: A node with no children.
- **Subtree**: A portion of a tree that itself forms a tree.
- **Height**: The longest path from the root to a leaf.
- **Depth**: The number of edges from the root to a node.

8.2 Binary Trees: Structure and Representation

A **binary tree** is a tree in which each node has at most two children, referred to as the left and right children. Binary trees are widely used due to their simple structure and efficiency in search and traversal operations.

Representation:

Each node in a binary tree is represented as:

```
struct Node {
  int data;
  struct Node* left;
  struct Node* right;
};
```

8.3 Binary Tree Traversals: Pre-order, Post-order, In-order

Traversal refers to visiting all the nodes in a tree in a specific order. The most common binary tree traversals are:

- **Pre-order**: Visit the root, then recursively traverse the left and right subtrees.
  Sequence: Root -> Left -> Right
- **In-order**: Recursively traverse the left subtree, visit the root, then traverse the right subtree.
  Sequence: Left -> Root -> Right
- **Post-order**: Recursively traverse the left and right subtrees, then visit the root.
  Sequence: Left -> Right -> Root

Example Program (In-order Traversal):

```
void inOrderTraversal(struct Node* node) {
  if (node == NULL) return;
  inOrderTraversal(node->left);
```

```
        printf("%d ", node->data);
        inOrderTraversal(node->right);
    }
```

8.4 Binary Search Trees: Concepts and Operations

A Binary Search Tree (BST) is a binary tree with the additional property that for each node:

- The left subtree contains values less than the node's value.
- The right subtree contains values greater than the node's value.

BSTs allow efficient searching, insertion, and deletion operations.

Operations:

Insertion: Traverse the tree to find the correct spot for the new node.
Search: Compare the target with each node, moving left or right depending on the value.
Deletion: Special cases arise when deleting a node with one or two children.

Example Program (Insertion in BST):

```
struct Node* insert(struct Node* node, int data) {
    if (node == NULL) {
        struct Node* newNode = (struct Node*)malloc(sizeof(struct Node));
        newNode->data = data;
        newNode->left = newNode->right = NULL;
        return newNode;
    }
    if (data < node->data) {
        node->left = insert(node->left, data);
    } else {
        node->right = insert(node->right, data);
    }
    return node;
}
```

8.5 Advanced Trees: AVL Trees, B-Trees, B+ Trees

AVL Trees are self-balancing binary search trees. After every insertion or deletion, AVL trees ensure that the heights of the two child subtrees of any node differ by at most one, maintaining balance.

B-Trees are balanced search trees used in databases and file systems. They allow nodes to have more than two children and maintain balance by ensuring that each node contains a range of keys.

B+ Trees are a variation of B-Trees where all leaf nodes are linked, making them ideal for database indexing.

8.6 Threaded Binary Trees: Concepts and Traversals

In threaded binary trees, pointers to NULL in traditional binary trees are replaced by pointers to the in-order successor or predecessor, allowing for efficient traversal without using a stack or recursion.

8.7 Applications of Trees

Trees are used in various fields such as:

Search Algorithms: Binary Search Trees and AVL Trees optimize searching.
File Systems: Directory structures are modeled using trees.
Expression Parsing: Expression trees represent mathematical expressions.
Databases: B-Trees and B+ Trees are used for indexing in databases.
Network Routing: Trees are used for efficient packet routing in network systems.

8.8 Glossary

Binary Tree: A tree where each node has at most two children.
Binary Search Tree: A binary tree where left children are less than the parent node, and right children are greater.

AVL Tree: A self-balancing binary search tree.
B-Tree: A balanced search tree with multiple children per node.
In-order Traversal: Traversing a tree by visiting the left subtree, root, and right subtree.
Threaded Tree: A binary tree where NULL pointers are replaced with pointers to in-order successors.

8.9 Summary

Trees: Hierarchical Data Structures with nodes connected by edges.
Binary Trees: Each node has at most two children (left and right).
Tree Traversals:
- **Pre-order**: Root -> Left -> Right.
- **In-order**: Left -> Root -> Right.
- **Post-order**: Left -> Right -> Root.

Binary Search Trees (BSTs):
- Left subtree contains values less than the node.
- Right subtree contains values greater than the node.

AVL Trees: Self-balancing binary search trees ensuring height balance.
B-Trees: Balanced trees allowing multiple children per node, used in databases.
B+ Trees: A variation of B-Trees with linked leaf nodes, ideal for indexing.
Threaded Binary Trees: NULL pointers are replaced with in-order successors for efficient traversal.
Applications of Trees: Used in search algorithms, file systems, expression parsing, databases, and network routing.

8.10 Previous year Unsolved Questions

1. What is a Tree? How does it differ from a Binary Tree? (IGNOU 2021)
2. How do you find depth and height of the tree? Give example. (RTU 2023-24)
3. Differentiate between trees and graph Data Structure (Pune University 2019)
4. Construct Binary Tree from following traversal. (MU 2022-23)
   In-order Traversal: DBHEIAFJCG
   Post order Traversal: DHIEBJFGCA
5. Explain the process of converting a Tree to a Binary Tree with an example. (IGNOU 2022)
6. Construct Huffman tree and determine the code for each symbol in the string "BCAADDDCCACACAC". (MU 2023-24)
7. Construct an expression tree for the expression (a + b / c) + ((d*e + f) / g). Give the outputs when you apply preorder and postorder traversals. (MU 2021-22)
8. In an AVL tree, the difference of height in left sub-tree and right-tree for every node is Tree. (MU 2022-23)
   A.) Zero
   B.) One
   C.) Atmost one
   D.) Atleast one
9. What is a Binary Tree? How does it differ from a tree? Write an algorithm for traversal of a Binary Tree. (IGNOU 2022)
10. Show the result of inserting 16, 18, 5, 19, 11, 10, 13, 21, 8, 14 one at a time into an initially empty AVL tree. (MU 2021-22)
    A. A hash table of size 10 uses linear probing to resolve collisions. The key values are integers and the hash function used is key%10. Draw the table that results after inserting in the given order the following values: 28, 55, 71, 38, 67, 11, 10, 90, 44, 9
    B. Write a program to implement Circular queue using an array.
    Write a program to convert the given decimal number to a binary number using stack Data Structure.

Exercises

Exercise 1 – Multiple Choice Questions

1. Which sorting algorithm has the best average time complexity for large datasets?
    - a) Bubble Sort
    - b) Selection Sort
    - c) Merge Sort
    - d) Insertion Sort
2. What is the worst-case time complexity of Quick Sort?
    - a) O(n^2)
    - b) O(n log n)
    - c) O(n)
    - d) O(log n)

Exercise 2 – True/False

1. Merge Sort has a time complexity of O(n log n) in all cases (best, average, worst).
2. Quick Sort is a stable sorting algorithm.

Exercise 3 – Fill in the blanks

1. The best-case time complexity of Bubble Sort occurs when the array is _______ sorted.
2. Quick Sort uses a pivot to partition the array and recursively sort the _______ and _______ subarrays.

Exercise 4- Fill in the blanks with two options

1. In Merge Sort, the array is divided into _______ halves, and then the sorted halves are _______ together.
2. Insertion Sort works by picking an element from the unsorted portion and inserting it into its correct position in the _______ part of the array until the entire array is _______.

Exercise 5- Rearrange the sentence

1. On / works / Merge / divide-and-conquer / a / technique / Sort.
2. Bubble / array / sorted / Sort / already / performs / best / when / is / the.

Exercise 6- Choose the Odd One Out

1. Which one is the odd one out?
    - A) Quick Sort
    - B) Heap Sort
    - C) Merge Sort
    - D) Bubble Sort
2. Which one is the odd one out?
    - A) Merge Sort
    - B) Radix Sort
    - C) Selection Sort
    - D) Counting Sort

Exercise 7- Jumble words

1. NOITCELECS-RTSO
2. ILQCUK-RTSO

Exercise 8- Match case

Column A

1. Quick Sort
2. Merge Sort
3. Insertion Sort
4. Selection Sort
5. Heap Sort

Column B
a) Divides the array into halves and merges
b) Selects a pivot and partitions the array
c) Builds a binary heap to sort the array
d) Repeatedly selects the smallest element
e) Inserts elements into their correct position

Exercise 9- Assertion – Reason

1. Assertion: Quick Sort has an average time complexity of O(n log n).
Reason: Quick Sort uses a pivot element to partition the array into smaller subarrays and recursively sorts them.
a) Both Assertion and Reason are correct explanation for Assertion.
b) Both Assertion and Reason but Reason is the correct explanation for Assertion.
c) Assertion is correct, but Reason is incorrect.
d) Assertion is incorrect, but Reason is correct.

Exercise 10- Read the questions given below and find the appropriate word in the grid provided.

B	I	N	A	R	Y	L	M	P
C	W	L	Q	P	L	E	A	F
D	M	T	S	N	I	R	J	X
H	I	B	U	R	V	T	W	Q
O	N	E	K	Z	A	G	L	A
L	E	A	F	B	S	H	K	C
P	J	G	Y	X	R	T	I	Z

Find the following words in the grid:
1. Binary
2. Leaf

Exercise 11- One- word

1. Which sorting algorithm has the worst-case time complexity of O(n^2)?
2. What is the time complexity of Merge Sort in the worst case?

Exercise 12- Small Answers

1. What is the difference between Merge Sort and Quick Sort?
2. Why is Insertion Sort more efficient on smaller arrays or nearly sorted arrays?

Exercise 13- Long Answers

1. Explain the working of Merge Sort and Quick Sort. Compare their time complexities and space complexities.
2. What is Heap Sort? Explain how it works and discuss its time complexity and space complexity.

Answers

Exercise 1-

1. c) Merge Sort, 2. a) O(n^2)

Exercise 2-

1. True, 2. False

Exercise 3-

1. Already, 2. left, right

Exercise 4-

1. two, merged, 2. sorted, sorted

Exercise 5-

1. Merge Sort works on a divide-and-conquer technique, 2. Bubble Sort performs best when the array is already sorted.

Exercise 6-

1. Bubble Sort, 2. Selection Sort

Exercise 7-

1. Selection Sort, 2. Quick Sort

Exercise 8-

1-B,2-A,3-E,4-D,5-C

Exercise 9-

1. b) Both Assertion and Reason are True, and Reason is the correct explanation of Assertion.

Exercise 11-

1. Quick Sort, 2. O(n log n)

Test Paper

Chapter-8
Tree

Time Duration: 30 Minutes **Maximum Marks: 25**

General Instructions:

1. The question paper consists of 12 questions and is divided into four sections, A, B, C and D.
2. All questions are compulsory.
3. Section A comprises MCQs, Fill in the blanks and True or False carrying one marks each.
4. Section B comprises VSAQs(very short answers questions) carrying two marks each.
5. Section C comprises SAQs(short questions) carrying four marks each.
6. Section D comprises long questions carrying five marks each.

SECTION-A

I. Multiple choice questions: **(1*2=2)**

1. Which sorting technique is based on the divide-and-conquer approach?
   a) Bubble Sort
   b) Merge Sort
   c) Selection Sort
   d) Insertion Sort
2. In which case does Bubble Sort perform the best?
   a) When the array is in reverse order
   b) When the array is already sorted
   c) When the array has all distinct elements
   d) It performs the same in all cases

II. Fill in the blanks: **(1*2=2)**

1. The space complexity of Merge Sort is _______ due to the extra space required for merging.
2. Heap Sort builds a binary _______ to sort the elements in an array.

III. True or False: **(1*2=2)**

1. Selection Sort is faster than Merge Sort for large datasets.
2. Insertion Sort has a time complexity of O(n^2) in the worst case.

SECTION-B

IV. Very Short answers type questions-I **(2*3=6)**

1. Which sorting algorithm uses a pivot to partition the array?
2. What type of sorting algorithm is Heap Sort?
3. Which sorting algorithm is best for nearly sorted arrays?

SECTION-C

V. Short answers type questions-II **(4*2=8)**

1. Explain the concept of stable and unstable sorting algorithms.
2. What is the main advantage of Merge Sort over Quick Sort?

SECTION-D

VI. Long answers type questions **(5*1=5)**

1. Describe Insertion Sort and explain its time complexity. When is Insertion Sort preferred over other sorting algorithms?

Chapter 9 - Graphs

In this chapter you will learn about:

Introduction to Graphs
Graph Terminology and Basic Concepts
Graph Representation
Graph Traversal Techniques
Minimum Spanning Trees
Shortest Path Algorithms
Applications of Graphs

Graphs are a key Data Structure in computer science used to model relationships between pairs of objects. A graph is made up of vertices (or nodes) and edges (or links) connecting them. Graphs are useful for representing networks, such as social networks, communication systems, and even geographic maps. This chapter explores various graph concepts, their representations, traversal techniques, and algorithms for solving common graph problems, such as finding minimum spanning trees and shortest paths.

9.1 Introduction to Graphs

A graph is a collection of vertices (nodes) and edges (connections between nodes). Graphs can be directed or undirected depending on whether the edges have a direction associated with them. Graphs can also have weighted edges, where each edge has a numerical value representing a cost, distance, or other attribute.

Types of Graphs:

- **Directed Graph (Digraph)**: The edges have a direction.
- **Undirected Graph**: The edges have no direction.
- **Weighted Graph**: Each edge is assigned a weight.
- **Unweighted Graph**: No weights are assigned to edges.

9.2 Graph Terminology and Basic Concepts

Key concepts in graph theory include:

- **Vertex (Node)**: A fundamental part of the graph where edges meet.
- **Edge (Link)**: A connection between two vertices.
- **Degree**: The number of edges incident to a vertex.
- **Path**: A sequence of vertices connected by edges.
- **Cycle**: A path where the starting and ending vertices are the same.
- **Connected Graph**: A graph where there is a path between any pair of vertices.
- **Acyclic Graph**: A graph without cycles.

9.3 Graph Representation: Adjacency Matrix, Adjacency List

Graphs can be represented in two primary ways:

- **Adjacency Matrix**: A 2D array where the rows and columns represent vertices, and the entries represent the presence (and possibly the weight) of an edge between two vertices.
  - **Space Complexity**: $O(V^2)$ where V is the number of vertices.
  - Efficient for dense graphs.

- **Adjacency List**: Each vertex maintains a list of adjacent vertices. This is more memory-efficient for sparse graphs.
  - **Space Complexity**: $O(V + E)$, where E is the number of edges.
  - Efficient for sparse graphs.

Example of Adjacency Matrix:

	0	1	2	3
0	0	1	0	0
1	0	0	1	1
2	0	1	0	1

3 0 0 0 0

Example of Adjacency List:

0 -> 1
1 -> 2, 3
2 -> 1, 3
3 ->

9.4 Graph Traversal Techniques: BFS and DFS

Traversal algorithms allow us to explore the vertices and edges of a graph in a systematic way.

Breadth-First Search (BFS): Explores all the neighbors of a node before moving on to their neighbors. BFS uses a queue to explore nodes level by level.

Time Complexity: O(V + E)

Example Program (BFS):

```
void BFS(int startVertex) {
  int visited[V];
  for (int i = 0; i < V; i++) visited[i] = 0;
  Queue q;
  enqueue(&q, startVertex);
  visited[startVertex] = 1;

  while (!isEmpty(&q)) {
    int vertex = dequeue(&q);
    printf("%d ", vertex);

    for (int i = 0; i < V; i++) {
      if (adjMatrix[vertex][i] == 1 && !visited[i]) {
        enqueue(&q, i);
        visited[i] = 1;
      }
    }
  }
}
```

Depth-First Search (DFS): Explores as far as possible along one branch before backtracking. DFS uses recursion or a stack.

Time Complexity: O(V + E)

Example Program (DFS):

```
void DFS(int vertex) {
  visited[vertex] = 1;
  printf("%d ", vertex);
  for (int i = 0; i < V; i++) {
    if (adjMatrix[vertex][i] == 1 && !visited[i]) {
      DFS(i);
    }
  }
}
```

9.5 Minimum Spanning Trees: Prim's and Kruskal's Algorithms

A Minimum Spanning Tree (MST) of a graph is a subset of the edges that connects all vertices together without any cycles and with the minimum possible total edge weight.

Prim's Algorithm: A greedy algorithm that grows the MST by adding the smallest edge that connects a vertex in the tree to a vertex outside the tree.

Time Complexity: $O(V^2)$ for adjacency matrix, O(E log V) for adjacency list with a priority queue.

Kruskal's Algorithm: A greedy algorithm that adds edges in increasing order of weight, ensuring that no cycles are formed.

Time Complexity: O(E log E)

9.6 Shortest Path Algorithms: Dijkstra's Algorithm

Dijkstra's Algorithm finds the shortest path from a source vertex to all other vertices in a weighted graph. It uses a priority queue to explore the closest vertex first.

Algorithm:

1. Initialize the distance to the source vertex as 0 and to all others as infinity.
2. Extract the vertex with the minimum distance from the priority queue.
3. Update the distance for its neighbors if a shorter path is found.
4. Repeat until all vertices are processed.Time Complexity: O(V log V + E)

9.7 Applications of Graphs

Graphs are used in a variety of real-world applications:

Social Networks: Modeling connections between individuals.
Routing and Navigation: Finding the shortest path in transportation and communication networks.
Dependency Resolution: Managing dependencies between tasks or processes.
Web Crawling: Traversing web pages using BFS or DFS.

9.8 Glossary

Vertex: A point in the graph.
Edge: A connection between two vertices.
Weighted Graph: A graph where edges have numerical values.
Adjacency Matrix: A 2D array representation of a graph.
Adjacency List: A list-based representation of a graph.
MST (Minimum Spanning Tree): A subset of edges that connect all vertices with minimal weight.

9.9 Summary

Graphs: A collection of vertices (nodes) and edges (links) used to represent relationships.
Graph Types: Directed, undirected, weighted, and unweighted graphs.
Graph Representations:

- **Adjacency Matrix**: 2D array representation, ideal for dense graphs.
- **Adjacency List**: List-based representation, ideal for sparse graphs.

Graph Traversals:

- **Breadth-First Search (BFS)**: Explores all neighbors level by level using a queue.
- **Depth-First Search (DFS)**: Explores as far as possible along one branch before backtracking using recursion or a stack.

Minimum Spanning Trees:

- **Prim's Algorithm**: Builds the MST by adding the smallest edge to the tree.
- **Kruskal's Algorithm**: Adds edges in increasing order of weight while avoiding cycles.

Shortest Path Algorithms:

- **Dijkstra's Algorithm**: Finds the shortest path from a source vertex in a weighted graph.

Applications: Social networks, routing, web crawling, and dependency resolution.

9.10 Previous year Unsolved Questions

1. Define Graph and explain various graph representation techniques. (MU 2022-23)
2. What are different ways of representing a Graph Data Structure on a computer? (MU 2023-24)
3. Represent any graph containing 5 Vertices and 7 Edges in Adjacency List Format. (RTU 2023-24)
4. Determine advantages and disadvantages of adjacent matrix representation for graphs. (RTU 2023-24)
5. What is meant by Minimum Cost Spanning Tree (MCST)? How can you find it? (IGNOU 2022)
6. Write Dijkstra's algorithm. (IGNOU 2022)
7. Explain graph traversing methods with pseudo code. (Pune University 2019)
8. How to represent graph using adjacency matrix and adjacency list? (Pune University 2019)

Exercises

Exercise 1 – Multiple Choice Questions

1. What is the time complexity of Linear Search in the worst case?
   a) O(log n)
   b) O(n log n)
   c) O(n)
   d) O(1)
2. Which searching technique is more efficient for sorted arrays?
   a) Linear Search
   b) Binary Search
   c) Hash Search
   d) Jump Search

Exercise 2 – True/False

1. Binary Search can be applied to unsorted arrays.
2. The worst-case time complexity of Binary Search is O(log n).

Exercise 3 – Fill in the blanks

1. Binary Search divides the array into _______ parts in each iteration.
2. Linear Search checks each element in the array one by one until the _______ element is found.

Exercise 4- Fill in the blanks with two options

1. Binary Search requires the array to be _______ and searches by repeatedly dividing the array into _______ parts.
2. Jump Search is a hybrid algorithm that jumps a fixed number of _______ and then performs a _______ search within the identified block.

Exercise 5- Rearrange the sentence

1. Efficient / is / Binary / for / arrays / Search / sorted.
2. Checks / element / one / search / each / by / search / linear / element / one.

Exercise 6- Choose the Odd One Out

1. Which one is the odd one out?
   A) Linear Search
   B) Binary Search
   C) Exponential Search
   D) Quick Sort
2. Which one is the odd one out?
   A) Jump Search
   B) Binary Search
   C) Merge Sort
   D) Interpolation Search

Exercise 7- Jumble words

1. ARIBYN-HCRSEA
2. RINEAL-HRCASE

Exercise 8- Match case

Column A

1. Linear Search
2. Binary Search
3. Jump Search

4. Exponential Search
5. Interpolation Search

Column B
a) Divides the array into two halves repeatedly
b) Searches by jumping a fixed number of steps
c) Checks each element one by one
d) Used when the size of the array is unknown
e) Estimates the position using a formula based on values

Exercise 9- Assertion – Reason

1. **Assertion:** Binary Search has a time complexity of O(log n) in the worst case.
   Reason: Binary Search reduces the search space by half after each comparison.
   a) Both Assertion and Reason are correct explanation for Assertion.
   b) Both Assertion and Reason but Reason is the correct explanation for Assertion.
   c) Assertion is incorrect, but Reason is incorrect.
   d) Assertion is correct, but Reason is correct.

Exercise 10- Read the questions given below and find the appropriate word in the grid provided.

V	E	R	T	E	X	H	J	K
A	B	C	I	W	F	G	P	O
L	R	G	E	D	G	E	Q	R
D	M	A	N	K	L	W	X	M
Z	O	P	A	G	R	A	P	H
T	R	A	C	Y	U	T	S	V
E	G	E	F	V	J	U	H	Z

Find the following words in the grid:

1. Vertex
2. Edge

Exercise 11- One- word

1. Which search algorithm works best for sorted arrays?
2. Which search algorithm checks elements one by one?

Exercise 12- Small Answers

1. What is the difference between Linear Search and Binary Search?
2. How does Binary Search work?

Exercise 13- Long Answers

1. Explain the working of Linear Search and Binary Search. Compare their time complexities and use cases.
2. What is Jump Search? How does it work, and in which situations is it more efficient than Linear Search?

Answers

Exercise 1-

1. c) O(n), 2. b) Binary Search

Exercise 2-

1. False, 2. True

Exercise 3-

1. Two, 2. target

Exercise 4-

1. sorted, two, 2. steps, linear

Exercise 5-

1. Binary Search is efficient for sorted arrays, 2. Linear Search checks each element one by one.

Exercise 6-

1. Quick Sort, 2. Merge Sort

Exercise 7-

1. Binary Search, 2. Linear Search

Exercise 8-

1-C,2-A,3-B,4-D,5-E

Exercise 9-

1. b) Both Assertion and Reason are True, and Reason is the correct explanation of Assertion.

Exercise 11-

1. Binary Search, 2. Linear Search

Test Paper

Chapter-9
Graphs

Time Duration: 30 Minutes **Maximum Marks: 25**

General Instructions:

1. The question paper consists of 12 questions and is divided into four sections, A, B, C and D.
2. All questions are compulsory.
3. Section A comprises MCQs, Fill in the blanks and True or False carrying one marks each.
4. Section B comprises VSAQs(very short answers questions) carrying two marks each.
5. Section C comprises SAQs(short questions) carrying four marks each.
6. Section D comprises long questions carrying five marks each.

SECTION-A

I. Multiple choice questions: **(1*2=2)**

1. Binary Search works efficiently only if the array is _______.
   a) Unsorted
   b) Sorted
   c) Partially sorted
   d) Reverse sorted
2. In Binary Search, how many times is the array divided at each step?
   a) 1
   b) 2
   c) 3
   d) 4

II. Fill in the blanks: **(1*2=2)**

1. Linear Search can be used for both sorted and unsorted arrays.
2. Jump Search is more efficient than Binary Search for large datasets.

III. True or False: **(1*2=2)**

1. In Exponential Search, we first find the range where the target element could be, then apply _______ Search in that range.
2. The time complexity of Linear Search in the worst case is _______.

SECTION-B

IV. Very Short answers type questions-I **(2*3=6)**

1. What is the worst-case time complexity of Binary Search?
2. Which search algorithm uses a fixed jump size to search faster?
3. Which search algorithm is used when the size of the array is unknown?

SECTION-C

V. Short answers type questions-II **(4*2=8)**

1. When would you prefer to use Jump Search over Linear Search?
2. Explain the basic concept of Exponential Search.

SECTION-D

VI. Long answers type questions **(5*1=5)**

1. Describe Exponential Search. How is it different from Binary Search, and what are its advantages?

Chapter 10 - Advance Data Structure and File Organization

In this chapter you will learn about:
Introduction to Hashing
Hash Functions
Collision Resolution Techniques
Open Addressing and Rehashing
Introduction to File Organization
Sequential, Indexed, and Hashed File Organizations
Storage Management Techniques
Memory Allocation
Garbage Collection and Compaction

In computer science, managing data efficiently is crucial for optimizing performance, especially in large-scale systems. Advanced Data Structures, such as hashing, and effective file organization techniques ensure quick data access, storage management, and optimal memory usage. This chapter dives deep into hashing, file organization, collision resolution techniques, memory allocation strategies, and garbage collection, providing an understanding of how modern systems store and retrieve information.

10.1 Introduction to Hashing

Hashing is a technique that transforms a given input (key) into a fixed-size value, typically an index, which can then be used to quickly access data in a hash table. Hashing is widely used for fast data retrieval in databases, caching systems, and file systems.

Hash Table: A Data Structure that stores key-value pairs, where a hash function maps each key to an index in the table.

Load Factor: The ratio of the number of elements to the total number of slots in the hash table, used to decide when to resize
the table.

10.2 Hash Functions: Concepts and Types

A hash function is an algorithm that converts an input (key) into a fixed-size integer, which serves as the index in the hash table. Good hash functions aim to distribute keys uniformly across the table to minimize collisions.

Properties of a Good Hash Function:

- **Deterministic**: The same input always produces the same output.
- **Efficient**: The hash function should be quick to compute.
- **Uniform Distribution**: Keys should be evenly distributed to avoid clustering.

Types of Hash Functions:

- **Division Method**: Key mod Table_Size.
- **Multiplication Method**: A constant multiplication of the key followed by a mod operation.
- **Universal Hashing**: A randomized hashing technique to reduce collisions.

10.3 Collision Resolution Techniques

Collisions occur when two keys are hashed to the same index. Several techniques are used to handle collisions:

- **Chaining**: Each slot in the hash table points to a linked list of all elements that hash to the same index.
- **Open Addressing**: When a collision occurs, the algorithm probes other slots in the table using a specific sequence (e.g., linear probing, quadratic probing).

10.4 Open Addressing and Rehashing

In open addressing, if a collision occurs, the hash table looks for the next available slot using a probing sequence.

Techniques in Open Addressing:

- **Linear Probing**: Move to the next available slot.

- **Quadratic Probing**: Move to slots at increasing intervals.
- **Double Hashing**: Use a second hash function to determine the probe sequence.

Rehashing involves resizing the hash table when the load factor becomes too high, typically by doubling the table size and re-inserting all elements using a new hash function.

10.5 Introduction to File Organization

File organization refers to how data is stored in files on disk. Efficient file organization is key to optimizing data retrieval and storage space.

File Organization Types:

- **Sequential File Organization**: Data is stored in a linear sequence, one record after another.
- **Indexed File Organization**: An index is created for faster access to records.
- **Hashed File Organization**: Data is stored based on the result of a hash function, allowing direct access to records.

10.6 Sequential, Indexed, and Hashed File Organizations

- **Sequential Organization**: Data is accessed in order; suitable for batch processing but slow for random access.
- **Indexed Organization**: Uses an index to allow quick random access to records without scanning the entire file.
- **Hashed Organization**: Records are stored in locations based on their hash value, providing fast direct access.

10.7 Storage Management Techniques

Storage management is essential to ensure efficient data access and organization, particularly in file systems. Techniques include:

- **Contiguous Allocation**: Files are stored in consecutive blocks on disk.
- **Linked Allocation**: Files are divided into blocks, and each block points to the next block in sequence.
- **Indexed Allocation**: An index block contains pointers to the data blocks of a file.

10.8 Memory Allocation: First Fit, Best Fit

Memory allocation strategies are crucial for efficiently using system memory:

- **First Fit**: The system allocates the first available block of memory that is large enough.
- **Best Fit**: The system allocates the smallest available block of memory that is large enough to minimize wasted space.

10.9 Garbage Collection and Compaction

Garbage collection is the process of automatically reclaiming memory that is no longer in use, preventing memory leaks in long-running programs.

- **Mark and Sweep**: Marks objects that are still in use and sweeps away unmarked objects.
- **Compaction**: After garbage collection, memory is compacted to eliminate fragmentation and improve memory allocation efficiency.

10.10 Glossary

- **Hashing**: A method of mapping data to a fixed-size index using a hash function.
- **Collision**: When two keys hash to the same index in a hash table.
- **Open Addressing**: A collision resolution method that probes for the next available slot.
- **File Organization**: The method used to store and organize data in files on disk.
- **Garbage Collection**: The process of reclaiming unused memory in programming environments.

10.11 Summary

- **Hashing**: A technique to map data to a fixed-size index using a hash function for fast data retrieval.
- **Hash Functions**: Algorithms that convert a key into an index; should be efficient and uniformly distribute keys.
- **Collision Resolution**: Techniques like chaining and open addressing handle cases where multiple keys hash to the same index.
- **Open Addressing**: Resolves collisions by probing other slots in the table (e.g., linear probing, quadratic probing).

Rehashing: Resizing the hash table and re-inserting elements when the load factor is too high.
File Organization: Methods to store and organize files on disk, including sequential, indexed, and hashed file organization.
Storage Management: Techniques like contiguous, linked, and indexed allocation optimize disk storage.
Memory Allocation: Strategies like First Fit and Best Fit allocate memory to minimize fragmentation.
Garbage Collection: Automatically reclaims unused memory; compaction reduces fragmentation after garbage collection.

10.12 Previous year Unsolved Questions

1. What is Breadth First Search? How does it differ from Depth First Search? (IGNOU-2022)
2. What is Hashing? Write a short note on it. (IGNOU-2022)
3. What is Storage Complexity? How does it differ from Time Complexity? (IGNOU-2022)
4. (a) What are the properties of an AVL tree? Explain the possible rotations that are possible on an unbalanced AVL tree.
   (b) Write Dijkstra's algorithm. (IGNOU-2022)
5. What is meant by *Big-O* notation? Explain with an example. (IGNOU-2022)
6. (a) What are various operations possible on Data Structures? (MU 2023-24)
   (b)What are different ways of representing a Graph Data Structure on a computer?
   (c) Describe Tries with an example.
   (d) Write a function in C to implement binary search.
7. What is hashing? What properties should a good hash function demonstrate? (MU 2023-24)

Exercises

Exercise 1 – Multiple Choice Questions

1. Which Data Structure is used in a priority queue?
   a) Stack
   b) Queue
   c) Heap
   d) Linked List
2. In a B-tree, what is the maximum number of children a node can have if the tree has an order of 4?
   a) 2
   b) 3
   c) 4
   d) 5

Exercise 2 – True/False

1. A B+ tree stores all keys in the internal nodes and values only in the leaf nodes.
2. Hash file organization always ensures sorted data storage.

Exercise 3 – Fill in the blanks

1. Trie is an advanced Data Structure used primarily for storing and searching ________in a dictionary-like format.
2. In Direct Access file organization, records are accessed using a _______ function, which computes the address of a record based on its key.

Exercise 4- Fill in the blanks with two options

1. In a B-tree, internal nodes store _______ to guide the search, while the leaf nodes contain _______.
2. Hashing is used for _______ access to records, while B+ trees are used for _______ access.

Exercise 5- Rearrange the sentence

1. Balanced / trees / AVL / maintain / height / through / rotation.
2. Each / at / tree / the / nodes / level / in / same / B / are.

Exercise 6- Choose the Odd One Out

1. Which one is the odd one out?
   A) AVL Tree
   B) B+ Tree
   C) Heap File
   D) Red-Black Tree
2. Which one is the odd one out?
   A) Sequential Access
   B) Direct Access
   C) Indexed Access
   D) Hash Tree

Exercise 7- Jumble words

1. EELVA-RTEE
2. TRIEXED-ACCESS

Exercise 8- Match case

Column A

1. B+ Tree
2. Hashing
3. AVL Tree

4. Sequential Access
5. Direct Access

Column B
a) Ensures logarithmic time for search in balanced trees
b) Stores keys in internal nodes and values in leaf nodes
c) Provides constant time complexity for direct access
d) Accesses records one after another
e) Uses a hash function to calculate the address of records

Exercise 9- Assertion – Reason

1. **Assertion:** B+ trees are more efficient than B-trees for range queries.
   Reason: In B+ trees, all data is stored in the leaf nodes, making sequential access to data faster.
   a) Both Assertion and Reason are correct explanation for Assertion.
   b) Both Assertion and Reason but Reason is the correct explanation for Assertion.
   c) Assertion is correct, but Reason is incorrect.
   d) Assertion is incorrect, but Reason is correct.

Exercise 10- Read the questions given below and find the appropriate word in the grid provided.

H	A	S	H	I	N	G	X	Y
T	R	E	E	W	Q	E	R	T
P	N	I	A	S	D	B	V	C
M	H	B	T	R	E	E	G	F
B	K	H	J	K	I	L	P	M
Z	I	O	T	B	N	W	H	T
S	X	T	G	R	A	T	W	Z
U	B	T	R	E	E	A	Q	V

Find the following words in the grid:
1. B-Tree
2. Hashing

Exercise 11- One- word

1. Which Data Structure is used to store sorted data and allows efficient range queries?
2. What is the maximum height difference allowed between subtrees in an AVL Tree?

Exercise 12- Small Answers

1. How does a B+ Tree differ from a B-Tree?
2. What is the purpose of balancing in an AVL Tree?

Exercise 13- Long Answers

1. Explain the structure and operations of a B+ Tree. Why is a B+ Tree preferred over a B-Tree for database indexing?
2. Describe the process of hashing in file organization. What are the main collision resolution techniques used in hashing?

Answers

Exercise 1-

1. c) Heap, 2. d) 5

Exercise 2-

1. True, 2. False

Exercise 3-

1. Strings, 2. hash

Exercise 4-

1. keys, data/records, 2. direct, sequential

Exercise 5-

1. AVL trees maintain balance through height rotation, 2. In a B-tree, the leaf nodes are at the same level.

Exercise 6-

1. Heap File, 2. Hash Tree

Exercise 7-

1. AVL Tree, 2. Indexed Access

Exercise 8-

1-b,2-E,3-A,4-D,5-C

Exercise 9-

1. b) Both Assertion and Reason are True, and Reason is the correct explanation of Assertion.

Exercise 11-

1. B+ Tree, 2. One

Test Paper
Chapter-10
Advance Data Structure and File Organization

Time Duration: 30 Minutes **Maximum Marks: 25**

General Instructions:

1. The question paper consists of 12 questions and is divided into four sections, A, B, C and D.
2. All questions are compulsory.
3. Section A comprises MCQs, Fill in the blanks and True or False carrying one marks each.
4. Section B comprises VSAQs(very short answers questions) carrying two marks each.
5. Section C comprises SAQs(short questions) carrying four marks each.
6. Section D comprises long questions carrying five marks each.

SECTION-A

I. Multiple choice questions: **(1*2=2)**

1. Which of the following file organization methods provides the fastest access to data?
   a) Sequential Access
   b) Direct Access
   c) Indexed Access
   d) Clustered Access
2. Which Data Structure allows for efficient range queries (e.g., finding all elements within a certain range)?
   a) AVL Tree
   b) B-tree
   c) Red-Black Tree
   d) Trie

II. Fill in the blanks: **(1*2=2)**

1. In a B+ tree, data records are stored only in the leaf nodes, while the internal nodes store the _______ for traversal.
2. AVL trees maintain balance by ensuring that the height difference between the left and right subtrees of any node is at most _______.

III. True or False: **(1*2=2)**

1. Heap file organization is the most efficient for sequential data retrieval.
2. In a B-tree, all leaf nodes are at the same level.

SECTION-B

IV. Very Short answers type questions-I **(2*3=6)**

1. Which file organization method provides constant time access using a hash function?
2. In which Data Structure are all the keys stored in internal nodes and data only in leaf nodes?
3. Which file organization technique reads data sequentially, one record after another?

SECTION-C

V. Short answers type questions-II **(4*2=8)**

1. How does Direct Access file organization work?
2. What is the advantage of using Hashing for file organization?

SECTION-D

VI. Long answers type questions: **(5*1=5)**

1. Compare and contrast Sequential Access and Direct Access file organization methods. What are the advantages and disadvantages of each?

Chapter 11 - Viva Voce

1. Q: What is a Data Structure?
   A: A Data Structure is a particular way of organizing and storing data in a computer so that it can be accessed and modified efficiently.
2. Q: Define an algorithm.
   A: An algorithm is a step-by-step procedure for solving a problem or accomplishing a task.
3. Q: Why are Data Structures important in programming?
   A: Data Structures are essential because they allow for efficient data management, enabling algorithms to run faster and use memory efficiently.
4. Q: Name some basic types of Data Structures.
   A: Arrays, linked lists, stacks, queues, trees, and graphs.
5. Q: What is the difference between an algorithm and a program?
   A: An algorithm is a plan or strategy for solving a problem, while a program is an implementation of an algorithm in a specific programming language.
6. Q: What is time complexity?
   A: Time complexity is a measure of the time an algorithm takes to complete as a function of the length of the input.
7. Q: Define Big O notation.
   A: Big O notation describes the upper bound of the time complexity, representing the worst-case scenario for an algorithm's execution time.
8. Q: What is space complexity?
   A: Space complexity is a measure of the amount of memory an algorithm uses relative to the input size.
9. Q: What is a linear Data Structure?
   A: A linear Data Structure organizes data in a sequential manner, such as arrays, linked lists, stacks, and queues.
10. Q: What is a non-linear Data Structure?
    A: A non-linear Data Structure does not store data in a sequence; examples include trees and graphs.
11. Q: What is an array?
    A: An array is a collection of elements stored in contiguous memory locations, accessible using indices.
12. Q: How does a linked list differ from an array?
    A: In a linked list, elements are stored in nodes connected by pointers, allowing for dynamic memory allocation, unlike arrays that use contiguous memory.
13. Q: What is a singly linked list?
    A: A singly linked list is a type of linked list where each node points to the next node in the sequence.
14. Q: What is a doubly linked list?
    A: A doubly linked list has nodes that contain pointers to both the next and previous nodes, allowing traversal in both directions.
15. Q: What are the advantages of using linked lists over arrays?
    A: Linked lists provide dynamic memory allocation, efficient insertions/deletions, and do not require contiguous memory.
16. Q: What is the disadvantage of using linked lists?
    A: Linked lists have higher memory overhead due to pointers and slower access time because elements are not contiguous.
17. Q: Explain the concept of circular linked lists.
    A: In a circular linked list, the last node points back to the first node, forming a circular structure.
18. Q: How do you insert an element in an array?
    A: Insert an element by shifting other elements if necessary to maintain the correct order.
19. Q: How is deletion handled in a linked list?
    A: Deletion involves changing pointers in nodes to remove the link to the node to be deleted.
20. Q: What is the time complexity of accessing an element in an array and in a linked list?
    A: Array access is O(1)O(1)O(1), while linked list access is O(n)O(n)O(n) for an element in a singly linked list.
21. Q: What is a stack?
    A: A stack is a linear Data Structure that follows the Last In, First Out (LIFO) principle.
22. Q: Name some common operations on a stack.
    A: Push, pop, peek (or top), and isEmpty.

23. Q: Describe the push operation in a stack.
A: Push adds an element to the top of the stack.
24. Q: Describe the pop operation in a stack.
A: Pop removes the top element from the stack.
25. Q: Give a real-life example of a stack.
A: A stack of plates in a cafeteria where you can only add or remove the top plate.
26. Q: What is a queue?
A: A queue is a linear Data Structure that follows the First In, First Out (FIFO) principle.
27. Q: Name some common operations on a queue.
A: Enqueue, dequeue, front, and isEmpty.
28. Q: Describe the enqueue operation in a queue.
A: Enqueue adds an element to the rear of the queue.
29. Q: Describe the dequeue operation in a queue.
A: Dequeue removes the element from the front of the queue.
30. Q: Give a real-life example of a queue.
A: A line of people waiting for a bus, where the first person in line is served first.
31. Q: What is recursion?
A: Recursion is a process where a function calls itself as part of its execution.
32. Q: What is a base case in recursion?
A: The base case is the condition under which the recursion stops.
33. Q: Give an example of a recursive algorithm.
A: Calculating the factorial of a number.
34. Q: What is a recursive function's time complexity generally dependent on?
A: It depends on the number of recursive calls made and the work done in each call.
35. Q: How does recursion relate to the call stack?
A: Each recursive call is pushed onto the call stack, and they are popped in reverse order when returning.
36. Q: What is sorting?
A: Sorting is the process of arranging data in a particular order, usually ascending or descending.
37. Q: Name some common sorting algorithms.
A: Bubble Sort, Selection Sort, Insertion Sort, Merge Sort, Quick Sort.
38. Q: Describe the Bubble Sort algorithm.
A: Bubble Sort repeatedly compares and swaps adjacent elements if they are in the wrong order.
39. Q: What is the time complexity of Quick Sort in the average case?
A: O(nlog n)O(n \log n)O(nlogn)
40. Q: Why is Merge Sort preferred over Bubble Sort for large datasets?
A: Merge Sort has better time complexity O(nlog n)O(n \log n)O(nlogn) compared to Bubble Sort's O(n2)O(n^2)O(n2) for large datasets.
41. Q: What is searching?
A: Searching is the process of finding a specific element in a Data Structure.
42. Q: Name two common searching algorithms.
A: Linear Search and Binary Search.
43. Q: What is the time complexity of Linear Search?
A: O(n)O(n)O(n)
44. Q: When can Binary Search be used?
A: Binary Search can be used on sorted arrays or lists.
45. Q: What is the time complexity of Binary Search?
A: O(log n)O(\log n)O(logn)
46. Q: What is a tree in Data Structures?
A: A tree is a hierarchical Data Structure with a root node and child nodes forming a parent-child relationship.
47. Q: What is a binary tree?
A: A binary tree is a tree Data Structure where each node has at most two children.
48. Q: What is a binary search tree (BST)?
A: A BST is a binary tree where each left child is less than the parent node, and each right child is greater.
49. Q: What is the height of a tree?
A: The height is the length of the longest path from the root to a leaf node.

Chapter 12 - Project And Case Study

Project: Library Management System
Objective:
The goal of this project is to develop a Library Management System (LMS) using the concepts of Data Structures and algorithms. This system will help students understand the practical applications of arrays, linked lists, stacks, queues, trees, and graphs in a real-world application. Students will also gain hands-on experience in creating efficient algorithms for data handling and retrieval.
Overview:
The Library Management System (LMS) will help manage a library's inventory, allowing for the addition, deletion, search, and organization of books. It will include user functions for issuing and returning books, managing a waiting list, and tracking book availability. Each function will be implemented using appropriate Data Structures covered in the book.

Key Components and Data Structures Used:

1. **Arrays and Linked Lists:**
   Arrays can store a list of books with fixed properties like titles and authors.
   Linked lists will manage the user data (e.g., borrower information) dynamically.
2. **Stacks:**
   A stack can be used to manage the recently issued or returned books, allowing the librarian to track the latest transactions efficiently.
3. **Queues:**
   A queue will be used to manage a waiting list for popular books. When a book is returned, the next person in the queue will get priority for issuance.
4. **Trees:**
   A binary search tree (BST) can be used to store the book titles in a sorted order, enabling efficient search operations. For instance, users can search for books by title.
5. **Graphs:**
   A graph structure can represent connections between different library sections. For example, if books are organized in various genres and sub-genres, a graph can help navigate the relationships between different sections.
6. **Sorting and Searching Algorithms:**
   Sorting techniques can be applied to display books in alphabetical order or by author name.
   Searching algorithms (linear and binary search) will help in finding books quickly.
7. **Advanced Data Structures (Hashing):**
   A hash table can be implemented to map user IDs to their checked-out books, allowing constant-time complexity for tracking user borrowing.

Steps to Develop the LMS:

1. **Create a Book Inventory:**
   Set up an array or linked list to hold book objects with attributes like title, author, ISBN, genre, and availability status.
2. **Implement a User Module:**
   Use a linked list to keep track of registered users and their details. Each user has a unique ID, name, and list of borrowed books.
3. **Book Issuance and Return System:**
   Implement stacks to manage the latest issued/returned books.
   When a book is issued, update the inventory status and track the transaction in a stack.
   If the book is not available, add the user to the waiting queue.
4. **Waiting Queue Management:**
   For high-demand books, maintain a queue of users waiting to borrow the book. Upon return, the book is issued to the next user in the queue.
5. **Book Search Functionality:**
   Use a binary search tree (BST) to store and search book titles.
   Implement binary search to efficiently locate a book by title.

6. **Category Navigation Using Graphs:**
   Create a graph to show connections between genres and sub-genres for easier navigation.
   Implement depth-first search (DFS) or breadth-first search (BFS) algorithms for exploring genres and finding related books.
7. **User Book Tracking with Hashing:**
   Use a hash table to map user IDs to borrowed books, allowing easy access to user-specific borrowing data.

Case Study: Real-World Application of Data Structures and Algorithms in E-commerce

Objective:

To examine how large e-commerce platforms use Data Structures and algorithms to efficiently handle inventory, customer orders, and product recommendations, with a focus on scalability, speed, and user experience.

Overview:

E-commerce websites like Amazon and eBay deal with millions of products, users, and transactions daily. Efficient data management is essential for handling large-scale inventory, search and filter options, recommendations, and checkout processes. This case study explores how Data Structures like arrays, linked lists, trees, graphs, and hash tables are employed in various parts of the e-commerce platform.

Core Applications and Data Structures Used:

1. **Inventory Management with Arrays and Hash Tables:**
   Products are stored in arrays or hash tables for fast retrieval.
   Hash tables map product IDs to details like name, price, and availability, enabling constant-time complexity for accessing product information.
2. **User Management with Linked Lists:**
   Customer data, including personal details, order history, and wish lists, are stored using linked lists for dynamic memory allocation.
   Each user is associated with a linked list of orders and wish-listed items, making it easier to add or remove items.
3. **Product Search and Filtering with Binary Search Trees (BST):**
   E-commerce websites allow users to search for products by various attributes, such as price, brand, and category. A BST organizes products by their names, allowing for efficient search and filtering.
4. **Recommendation System with Graphs:**
   Graphs are used to represent connections between different products, categories, or user interactions.
   For example, a "Customers who bought this also bought..." recommendation relies on graph traversal, where similar products are connected by edges.
5. **Order Processing with Queues:**
   A queue system processes customer orders, ensuring each order is handled in a first-come, first-served manner.
   Once an order is placed, it enters a queue for payment processing, packaging, and shipping.
6. **Transaction History with Stacks:**
   A stack is used to track the most recent transactions, allowing users to view their latest purchases quickly.
   If a user wants to view their order history, the system can pop the stack to retrieve recent orders.
7. **Advanced Data Structures (Heap for Priority Recommendations):**
   A max-heap is used to display top products based on ratings, views, or sales. This provides a quick way to highlight popular products.

Conclusion:

Data Structures and algorithms are crucial for building a fast, scalable, and user-friendly e-commerce platform. With millions of items in the inventory and thousands of daily transactions, e-commerce platforms rely on efficient algorithms to manage data, track orders, handle user searches, and recommend products. This case study illustrates how core concepts like arrays, linked lists, stacks, queues, trees, graphs, and hashing techniques play a vital role in creating a seamless shopping experience.

Chapter 13 - Sample Exam Paper

Time Duration: 3 Hours **Maximum Marks: 100**

General Instructions:

1. The question paper consists of 12 questions and is divided into four sections, A, B, C and D.
2. All questions are compulsory.
3. Section A comprises MCQs, Fill in the blanks and True or False carrying one marks each.
4. Section B comprises VSAQs(very short answers questions) carrying two marks each.
5. Section C comprises SAQs(short questions) carrying four marks each.
6. Section D comprises long questions carrying five marks each.

SECTION-A

I. Multiple choice questions: **(5*2=10)**

1. What is the worst-case time complexity of the Quick Sort algorithm?
   a) O(n log n)
   b) $O(n^2)$
   c) O(n)
   d) $O(n^3)$
2. Which Data Structure is used for implementing recursion?
   a) Queue
   b) Heap
   c) Stack
   d) Linked List

II. Fill in the blanks: **(5*2=10)**

1. The time complexity of the best-case scenario for sorting an array using the Merge Sort algorithm is ___________.
2. In a graph, a ___________ is a sequence of vertices in which each pair of consecutive vertices is connected by an edge.

III. True or False: **(5*2=10)**

1. The time complexity of searching an element in a Hash Table is O(1) on average.
2. Depth First Search (DFS) of a graph always visits all nodes in breadth-first order.

SECTION-B

IV. Short answers type questions-I **(10*3=30)**

1. What are Arrays? Write an algorithm to multiply two matrices.
2. What is Binary Search? Write an algorithm for it.
3. Convert the following expression to postfix: (a + b) / (c – d)

SECTION-C

V. Short answers type questions-II **(20*2=20)**

1. (a) What are the properties of an AVL tree? Explain the possible rotations that are possible on an unbalanced AVL tree.
   (b) Write Dijkstra's algorithm.
2. What is Breadth First Search? How does it differ from Depth First Search?

SECTION-D

VI. Long answers type questions **(20*1=20)**

1. (a) What is Breadth First Search? How does it differ from Depth First Search?
   (b)What is Hashing? Write a short note on it.